TROUBRIDGE

PETER LAWRANCE

TROUBRIDGE

AN ALBATROSS BOOK

Published in Australia and New Zealand by
Albatross Books Pty Ltd
PO Box 320, Sutherland
NSW 2232, Australia
in the United States of America by
Albatross Books
PO Box 131, Claremont
CA 91711, USA
and in the United Kingdom by
Lion Publishing plc
Peter's Way, Sandy Lane West
Oxford OX4 5HG, England

First edition 1995

National Library of Australia
Cataloguing-in-Publication data

Lawrance, Peter
Troubridge

ISBN 0 7324 1029 0

I.Title

A823.3

Cover illustration: Michael Mucci
Printed and bound by McPherson's Printing Group, Victoria

Contents

To Karmen

1

A shriek

THE CAVE WAS ROUND, a black opening high in the granite wall of the cliff. Like an empty eye-socket, it stared blindly across a rocky gorge towards rugged walls on the other side. It was overhung by a looming brow of rock that cast a black shadow, sharp-edged in the harsh summer light. The cave was hard to see unless you knew exactly where to look, but Shaun could pick it out; he knew it well. An angry sun glared, unblinking, from the sweating face of the sky, causing the rocks to glitter and ripple in the tortured air.

A figure clung to the side of the cliff below the cave. Even from this distance, Shaun knew it was Jamie. He could not say how he knew; he just knew. Jamie must have slipped and he now hung by his fingertips, legs kicking helplessly above the drop, pleading eyes turned upward. A group of figures stepped forward from the back of the cave and they seemed to be discussing Jamie and his plight. Strangely, Shaun seemed to have become one of them, no longer an onlooker. His sandy hair showed clearly against the darkness behind.

'He won't fit,' said Rick. 'There's no room for him up here.' Shaun knew it was a lie: the cave was easily large enough for all of them. Rick spoke again. 'He doesn't belong here, does he? He'd be out of place.'

Shaun heard his own voice, sounding weak and unconvincing, saying, 'If we don't help him, he'll fall.'

Rick was half a head taller than Shaun, dark-haired and handsome, without the freckles Shaun hated on his own face. He had a brilliant Tom Cruise smile that melted girls in their tracks and deep, guarded eyes that told other boys who was boss. Now, he turned those eyes upon Shaun. 'He'll fall anyway. If you try to help him, he'll take you down, too.'

'Yes,' Shaun agreed, relieved to have the decision taken out of his hands, 'I guess you're right.'

As he spoke, Jamie gave a terrified shriek and disappeared from view. Shaun could hear Jamie's body bumping and clattering on the loose rocks at the base of the cliff. It seemed to go on for a long time, the banging and knocking sounds echoing across the steep-sided valley.

He frowned. Some of the noises sounded more like cupboards opening and closing, cutlery tinkling in a drawer. The dream faded and, waking, he recognised the tinny resonance of the intercom on his desk at the other side of his small bedroom.

2

The intercom mystery

IT WAS ONE OF THOSE WIRELESS INTERCOMS. You know, you plug it into the power point in one part of the house and you can talk to someone who has one plugged in somewhere else. In Shaun's case, it was a bit different. He was boarding with the Walkers and the conversations took place between their kitchen and his granny-flat at the bottom of the garden.

He groaned and turned over in bed, pulling the pillow around his ears, but he could still hear the clattering of dishes and Mrs Walker's voice sounding hollow and far away. They had bumped the 'talk' button again and locked it on without noticing. Rats! He could turn it off at his end, of course, but that would mean getting out of bed and crossing the cold vinyl floor, chilled by the winter air. Apart from freezing his feet, it would mean feeling guilty when he saw, spread out on the desk, the Geography assignment that would not be handed up tomorrow if he went skateboarding with Rick and Jason today. Rats.

Shaun groaned again and released the pillow, rolling over the other way to glare at the clock on his bedside table. Eight fifteen. Well, it was about time he got up anyway. He counted backwards from ten and, with one more monumental groan to demonstrate what a superhuman effort he was making, he erupted from beneath the bedclothes and sprinted to the bathroom. He danced on the frigid tiles while the water got warm enough for comfort, then plunged gratefully under the shower.

As the hot water cascaded over his head and body, Shaun's brain gradually came to life. He struggled for a while with his conscience over the Geography assignment, but in the end decided to put off the choice until he had eaten breakfast and phoned Rick to see if Spud was coming to the ramp.

Spud. He hadn't got up the nerve yet to ask what her real name was. Spud could not really be described as pretty, with her turned-up nose and severely cropped hair. She dressed like a boy and hung around with her brother and his friends more often than with other girls, but she was female enough to interest Shaun more than a little. She could handle a skateboard better than he could, which was a bit intimidating, but then he had never used one before he came down from his outback home to go to school in Adelaide.

Yes, he thought, if Spud was coming, he would go to the skate ramp and try to complete the assignment later. If she wasn't, he would do some work on the assignment during the day and maybe wander over to visit Rick and his sister around five o'clock in the hope that he would be invited to stay for dinner. He grunted, well satisfied with the wisdom of this decision, and turned off the water.

In the bedroom, Shaun crossed to the intercom that had wakened him and glared at it. There was no-one talking or making a noise now, but he thought he could still discern the echoey background sound the thing made when the channel was open. He pressed the call button a couple of times but nothing happened, so he shrugged his shoulders and started pulling on his clothes. He was tying his second shoelace when, thin-sounding but otherwise as clear as a bell, a woman's voice said, 'Ginny! Call your father inside, will you? His breakfast's getting cold.'

Shaun looked up, startled. That wasn't Mrs Walker. He sat on the edge of the bed and stared across the room at the intercom. The voice continued after a moment, but the speaker had moved away and her words were fainter, obscured by bumping and scraping sounds. Shaun was really puzzled now. Who was the mystery woman in the Walkers' kitchen? And who on earth was this Ginny she was talking to? He quickly finished tying his shoes and went to investigate.

Winter was drawing to a close in the Adelaide Hills. Opening the door to the garden, Shaun found the world grey and damp with fog. The dripping treetops were lost from sight and everything sounded muted and distant. Although the house was only twenty metres up the hill, it was all but invisible; just a ghostly shape in the mist.

The kitchen was empty. Shaun could see that as he looked through the glass panel in the back door. He was surprised to find the door locked and used his key. It was not until he stood in front of the intercom mounted on the wall beside the phone — an intercom that not only had its talk button in the normal receiving position, but was not even switched on — that it dawned on him.

Sunday. The Walkers would have been at church since eight o'clock. Shaun used to go with them when he first arrived — the friendly atmosphere and the familiar services comforted him during the first lonely months away from home — but, since he had started hanging around with Rick and the others, he had attended less and less often and finally stopped altogether.

Then what about the voice on the intercom? Shaun's scalp began to prickle as he made his way cautiously from room to room. He began to feel slightly silly in the end, as he tiptoed up to each doorway and peered around it, but surely there had been someone in the house? Well, there wasn't now; he had the place to himself. He thought about the puzzle over corn flakes and orange juice. If the intercom could work between the house and the granny-flat, maybe it could work between different houses. Perhaps, he concluded, he had been listening to a conversation in someone else's kitchen.

His train of thought was interrupted by the telephone. It was Rick. Was he coming to the skate ramp? Maybe; who else was going to be there? Spud's name was mentioned. Yes, he would meet them at the station at ten.

One of Mrs Walker's few rules was that he should rinse his own breakfast dishes rather than leave them for her to wash. As he stood at the sink, he stared through the window at the low cloud which lay eerily about two metres off the ground. Tree trunks stood like a line of spectral sentries along the drive-way, fading headless into the wet, grey blanket.

The Walkers were kind, but he just couldn't feel at home here. It wasn't the house, it was the whole city. Okay, so Blackwood was a nice enough part of Adelaide — the tree-clad hills made it almost like living in the country — but the winter was chilling and damp rather than crisp and cool, and he found the stifling summer heat oppressive.

At home on Turtleshell Station, although it was customary to curse the dust and the drought, Shaun loved it best when the sun burned with exuberant fury and the dry wind sucked the very sweat from your pores. It was what he was born to; it was what he was made for. He had tried hard to make the best of his time in exile — after all, he had three more years of school to go if his parents had their way — but he knew he didn't belong.

That had been the real pain of it, the feeling of not belonging, of being left out of the friendship that everyone else seemed to enjoy. For the first six months he had felt like a stranger in a strange land, as though everyone around him spoke a language he could not quite understand and shared jokes he could not quite comprehend.

Then, gradually, he had discovered the secrets. He started hanging around on the fringes of Rick's group before school and at lunchtime. He laughed when they laughed, whether he got the point or not. He learned the right words and, just as important, when and how to say them. Once, at the hairdresser's, he plucked up the courage to ask for a haircut like the kid in the next chair.

The breakthrough had come when Rick discovered that this boy from the bush could drive a truck and ride a motorbike and weld. From then on, Rick's support guaranteed Shaun the acceptance of the others. Shaun was grateful for this, although he was a bit uncomfortable with the feeling of indebtedness towards Rick.

Rick, for his part, somehow managed to make it clear that a place in the group, granted at his word, could be withdrawn just as easily.

But Shaun had learned the most important lesson from a boy called James Cragg. Jamie had be-friended Shaun from the start, sensing that he felt lost in the throngs of kids at the school. At first Shaun had been grateful, but gradually Jamie had become an embarrassment. He was small for his age. He wore glasses and didn't ride a skateboard. He handed in assignments on time and the week he admitted he went to church was the week Shaun decided to stop altogether. Rick had a word for kids like that: *losers.*

As Shaun began to orbit closer to Rick's crowd, he had realised that Jamie was a liability; by associ-ating with a loser, he was in danger of being labelled the same. So he began to cut him off, found excuses to stop visiting him and avoided him in the schoolyard.

Jamie had tried to follow Shaun into the group, but they had made fun of him, calling him 'Cragg the Scragg' and chasing him off with shouts of abuse whenever he approached. Shaun had not actually participated in this himself, but he made no move to stop it, either. He sensed that Jamie was going down; there was nothing he could do to prevent it and he had a lot to lose by becoming entangled, so he just let nature take its course. It was sad, but that, Shaun had learned, was how things worked.

Jamie eventually gave up trying to join the group, but it was too late; the harassment continued. He endured until the end of the year before begging his parents to send him to another school. Shaun soothed his conscience with the thought that it was probably for the best. Jamie would be happier somewhere else. Now, though, remembering his dream, Shaun paused in the act of hanging up the tea-towel, guilt niggling at the pit of his stomach. Nothing I did would have made any difference, he told himself, shaking off the feeling as he let himself out the back door and locked it behind him.

There were six of them in the group now: Rick and his sister Spud, Jason, Dave and his girlfriend Nina, and Shaun. They were all in the same year at school, except for Spud who was a year younger, and they spent a lot of their spare time together.

The train trip down to the ramp was a riot; they always had fun when they got together. Being in a bunch like that gave Shaun confidence he had never possessed outside the boundaries of the sheep station where he had grown up, and he jostled and called out with the rest as they made their way to their favourite seats at the very back of the carriage. Jason claimed to know the writers of all the tags adorning the walls, ceiling and seats, and treated everyone including the other passengers to a loud lecture on the merits of different brands of spray paint and marking pens.

Once at the ramp, any onlooker could easily have understood how the group was organised. Rick was the leader and could skate better than any of them. Jason came next, then Dave, then at the bottom of the pile, Shaun. Nina didn't skate: she just looked on adoringly while Dave did his stuff. Spud was the exception. Her skill with a skateboard should have ranked her second, but she didn't seem to care about that kind of thing and, since she was a girl, and the youngest at that, nobody thought of offering it to her.

They had to take turns with several other skaters, so it was a while before Shaun got a go. He had been practising on the long concrete slope of the Walkers' drive and he thought he was getting quite good now. His first turn on the ramp confirmed to him that he really had the hang of it at last; he dropped in from the top of the half-pipe and swept energetically back and forth eight times before he overbalanced. However, he managed to keep his feet and it looked almost as though he had stopped on purpose to give someone else a turn. His performance earned him a shout of encouragement from Dave, a benevolent punch on the arm from Rick and, unless he imagined it, an admiring look from Spud.

All right! Next time he would really show them something.

He certainly did. When his turn came around again, he dropped in with an accomplished flourish yelling, 'Watch this!' They all watched, but it was Spud's eyes he could really feel as he pumped the board higher and higher with each pass across the ramp. This was it! He flexed his knees at the bottom of the pipe and pushed off. The wheels cleared the lip at the top of the ramp but, as he groped desperately for the side-rail to keep the board in contact with his feet, it spun away from him and he came crashing down painfully on his left hip, skinning his elbow on the surface of the ramp as he slid ungracefully to the bottom.

It was difficult to tell what hurt most, his hip, his elbow or his pride, as the audience burst into howls of laughter:

'Great trick, Shaun!'

Only Spud came to his aid, but Shaun was embarrassed enough already without having to be helped up by someone's sister. Forcing himself to grin as his eyes stung with unwelcome tears, he struggled to his feet, retrieved the errant board and managed to get off the ramp before Spud reached him with her outstretched hand.

He was too busy with his own injuries to notice the hurt in her face as she watched his retreating back.

3

A painful decision

SHAUN WAS THOROUGHLY DISGRUNTLED. Mr Anderson had chewed his ear in Geography about the unfinished assignment and now he slumped in his chair, drawing on the back of his hand, while Ms Perling's Maths lesson flew over his head in a perplexing tangle of polynomials and quadratic equations.

The bell sounded and twenty-three students leapt to their feet, snapping books shut and slamming chairs against the desks. They shoved and shouted their way into the corridor where clashing locker doors announced that the morning's lessons were over. Shaun took his time gathering up his books and getting his lunch. Ms Perling smiled gratefully at him as he righted a fallen chair on his way out of the room.

He was still smarting from yesterday's humili-ation. It made him wince to think of it; what an idiot he must have looked, showing off like that and then falling flat on his face. His backside, actually. It still hurt like hell when he moved the wrong way. He dawdled on his way into the yard, hoping that Rick and Jason and the others would have moved off to some other part of the school grounds and he would not have to meet up with them. Spud often joined them at lunchtime and he was not yet ready to face her again.

He might as well not have bothered. There they all were, in a bunch a few steps from the door. They saw him as soon as he left the building and started calling to him: 'Where's your board, Shaun? How about a demonstration!'

Shaun tried to think of a smart comment to disarm their jibes, something that would confirm him as a proper member of the group instead of a loser, a misfit who couldn't even handle a skateboard. 'Round the world in eighty days,' he said, smiling ruefully and rubbing his backside. He had no idea what it meant or how the others would take it but, to his immense relief, Rick laughed and the others joined in.

Rick walked towards him, rubbing his own rear and repeating the joke, and Shaun knew he was safe: if Rick liked it that much, the others would, too. Spud wandered over and Shaun carefully joined in the clowning for the next few minutes, pretending to ignore her, but all the while snatching glances out of the corner of his eye to see if she was looking.

Suddenly, in the middle of some hilarious story or other, Jason stopped. His eyes were focused on the far side of the yard. 'Hey, what's that coon doing over there?'

They all looked, and Shaun saw, clutching the top of the low cyclone-wire fence and peering in from the street, an Aboriginal boy about their own age.

In Shaun's family, the word was simply 'Aboriginal', but that didn't seem to fit the tone of this conversation. There was another word, though. He had heard it at football matches and outside pubs. 'Coon?' he laughed. 'Where I come from we call 'em boongs.'

Dave crosssed his eyes and pretended to hit himself on the head. 'Boongggg, boongggg!' Jason doubled up laughing, and Shaun was greatly pleased to have made such a humorous contribution.

Rick interrupted the entertainment. 'Who's he waving at? Hey, Shaun, you come from coon country. Perhaps he's waving at you. Maybe he knows you!'

'Wouldn't think so,' answered Shaun swiftly. 'Never saw him before.' He turned away from the fence and the conversation swept on to other topics. When he glanced around again, the boy was gone.

Later, during Tech Studies, Shaun could not get the incident out of his mind. He made what his father would have called a 'dog's dinner' of the sheet metal pencil case he was fabricating. He knew who the boy at the fence was, all right. He had known at the time, he admitted to himself, so why had he pretended not to?

There was no sign of the boy when the tide of students swept out the gate after school. Shaun and his friends straggled up Shepherd's Hill Road, griping about teachers and parents and laying plans for the weekend four long days away.

That night, Shaun dreamt again about the cave on Turtleshell Station. This time, though, it was not James Cragg who clung to the shimmering rock face, but an Aboriginal boy with ragged black curls showing from under Shaun's second-best hat. Shaun wanted to reach out and help him but, once again, Rick's voice in his ear and those commanding eyes convinced him that things were better left as they were. The boy fell, but Shaun never heard him hit the bottom: he awoke in the dark, trembling, with that horrible scream ringing in his ears.

Next day, at lunchtime, the boy was back at the fence. This time it was clear he was trying to attract someone's attention: he looked straight at them and waved energetically.

'You sure you don't know him?' asked Jason, accusingly. 'None of us has an Abo for a friend, so it must be you.'

Shaun hesitated. 'Could be Sam Dobson,' he mumbled at last.

Rick was exultant. 'Now we're getting somewhere! Go and see what he wants. Coons get lost in the big city, you know.'

'Maybe he's out of wichetty grubs,' suggested Dave with a smirk.

In the face of the barrage of jesting from his friends, Shaun realised he had no choice. His best bet would have been to make another joke of it, but he couldn't think of anything funny to say. In the end, he just muttered, 'He doesn't eat wichetty grubs.'

As he crossed the yard, Shaun recalled that dangerous summer when they had met. Sam's father had been employed for a time as a station hand on Turtleshell, moving his family into the workman's cottage near the old homestead. The two boys had clashed at first, but they had gone through a pretty tough time together and come out of it firm friends.

No, there was nothing wrong with Sam. He was a good kid, but he belonged to a different world from the one Shaun shared with his school friends, another life that he had almost forgotten. The thought of juggling two worlds was more than he could cope with just then.

It wasn't fair; he shouldn't have just popped up out of the blue like that. Sam's sudden appearance had caught Shaun unawares; he sensed that his hard-won place in Rick's circle was suddenly in doubt and the idea alarmed him.

'You took your time.' Sam was trying to grin, but his eyes held the same wary, hunted look they possessed when Shaun had first met him. Shaun glanced over his shoulder and saw that the others were watching him with interest. 'What's the matter?' Sam continued. 'Afraid someone might see you talking to a blackfeller?'

Shaun opened his mouth to defend himself, but thought better of it. 'What are you doing here?' he asked instead. 'I thought you were in Leigh Creek.'

Sam became serious. 'I was, but I took off.' For a second he seemed about to explain, but instead he just looked down at the ground and Shaun didn't push it.

'Staying with your uncle?'

'Well, that's the thing. I was going to, but he's not there. The old bloke who lives in the same place says he thinks he might have gone down to the South East, but he's not sure. Also thought he might have gone to see his brother in Port Augusta. All he knows for sure is that he isn't in Adelaide.'

'Well, where are you staying, then?'

'Nowhere really. I tried to sleep on a seat at the station last night, but the cops hassled me and I had to move on.'

Shaun squirmed inwardly at the unspoken rebuke and studied his feet, kicking at the ground with the toe of one shoe. When he looked back up, it was with more sympathetic eyes, and he saw the weariness behind the front of bravado Sam was trying to maintain. 'You can stay with me,' he offered. 'I'll have to ask the Walkers, but they're pretty nice; I'm sure it'd be okay with them.'

Sam jumped to the defensive. 'Hey,' he retorted, 'I didn't ask for any favours, did I? I'll be all right.'

'No, you won't. Besides,' Shaun grinned suddenly, 'we could have some fun together.' He could hear the others calling to him. 'Look, I've got to go. Know where the Pizza Hut is?' Sam shook his head and Shaun pointed. 'Just head up that road there and turn left at the roundabout. You can't miss it. Meet me there after school.'

Rejoining the others, he was assailed with questions. 'Who is he? Where do you know him from?' Rick's voice came in above the others: 'What did the Abo want, Shaun?'

Shaun's conscience was giving him a hard time and his patience was wearing thin. 'Give it a rest, Rick. He's a friend of mine. What difference does it make if he is an — if he's black or white? Anyway, he's come down from Leigh Creek for. . .' he searched for a suitable word '. . .a holiday.'

Dave's eyes grew wide with mock amazement. 'Ooh! A holiday! He's a pretty civilised coon, then, is he?'

'Holiday, nothing,' laughed Rick. 'He's on walkabout. That's right, isn't it Shaun? He's on his way to a corroboree.'

Shaun looked across the yard to where Sam, appearing lonely and defenceless in the distance, was still gazing in from outside the school boundary. That was when it happened. He could still see the school buildings and the asphalt-paved grounds, but superimposed over them in his mind's eye were the angular crags of the Turtleshell Range and the gaping mouth of the cave where a boy's life hung in the balance. At that moment, just as in his dream, the choice was his and, as he made it, he had the strangest feeling that he was deciding his own fate as much as Sam's. He couldn't keep quiet any longer.

'Oh, shut your face! What would you know anyway? Keep talking like that and you're looking for trouble!'

Rick pretended to cringe in fear, then his lip curled. 'What's the matter with you? Ashamed to be a white man or something?'

Shaun turned and looked hard at Rick. He suddenly realised he had never really liked him. 'Yes,' he answered. 'Sometimes.'

As Shaun walked away, with his shoulders hunched and his hands thrust deep into his pockets, he knew that a door had just closed. It had taken him a long time to win Rick's acceptance and now he had thrown it all away. Looking back on it, though, he wondered whether the struggle had been worthwhile in the first place.

For months, he had pretended to like music that really sounded awful to him, laughed at jokes that weren't funny and had his hair cut in a style which, even at the time, he thought looked stupid. He had stood by and done nothing while Rick, Jason and Dave had hounded Jamie Cragg out of the school. His father had a word for it: *spineless*.

Now Sam had arrived and reminded him of how life used to be, what a real friendship was. It had felt good to tell Rick what he really thought; it had broken the spell. It was like waking from a bad dream.

Shaun wanted to be alone, so the footsteps behind him were unwelcome. The voice, though, surprised him. It was Spud's. 'Hey, wait!' He slowed while she caught up and walked beside him. 'Don't take any notice of Rick,' she said. 'He doesn't really mean it.'

'Doesn't he?'

'He's just being stupid. You know Rick; he gets together with the others and he thinks he has to act tough or they won't like him. Pretty immature, really.' She paused and they walked together in silence. Shaun should have been pleased: he was walking and talking alone with her. All he could think of, though, was how weak and transparent he must have seemed to her all those months while he flattered and grovelled his way into Rick's circle.

'You're different,' Spud continued. 'You know what you think and you're not afraid to say it. You don't feel you have to act big to prove a point.' Shaun was too astounded to speak. He just grunted. His bruised rump told a completely different story; it still ached with every step.

They had reached the far side of the yard by now and Shaun had recovered enough to realise he should try to capitalise on this unexpected opportunity. After all his efforts to attract Spud's attention, funny it should happen like this. . . He turned and tried to lean nonchalantly against the fence. The effect was spoilt, though, by the discovery that he was still clutching the tomato sandwich Mrs Walker had made him for lunch. Some time in the past twenty minutes — he could not remember just when — he must have tightened his grip on it considerably. It was thoroughly mangled and, although it was wrapped in plastic, the juice was leaking out into his hand.

The bell rang again. 'P.E. — gotta go!' Spud called over her shoulder as she trotted off towards the gym. The moment was lost. With a sigh, Shaun turned and made his way towards the main buildings, dropping the dead sandwich into a bin on the way and attempting to de-juice his fingers with a handkerchief.

There was no way to escape from the others on the way home: they all walked and all in the same direction. He lingered inside the grounds, hoping that they would not wait for him. Some hope. Rick spotted him as he reached the gate. 'Hey, Shaun! Come here!'

'Why?'

'Because I said so!'

Shaun's solitary upbringing had taught him to be satisfied with his own company, so he had never feared being on his own. Having friends turn against him, though, was different. 'Get lost,' he muttered, but they didn't.

Jason and Dave moved forward on either side, crowding him against the fence, while Rick advanced until Shaun could smell the cigarette smoke in his hair. They glared at each other, Shaun reading clearly in Rick's face the authority he had to decide people's destiny. The warning edge to Rick's voice was unmistakable. 'Listen, loser, I didn't like the way you spoke to me today. It wasn't friendly, was it?'

Shaun had had enough. He felt suddenly dangerous. 'I didn't like the way you spoke about Sam. He's worth two of you, I reckon.' Jason shook him, pushing him painfully back against the fence, but he hardly noticed; instead, he was fascinated by the subtle shift in Rick's eyes. It was as though a blind had lifted for a second, allowing Shaun to glimpse a secret room. But in the next instant the mask was back, the shutters firmly in place, leaving Shaun wondering if he had imagined Rick's fear. . .

'Get him out of here!' was the order and, in instant obedience, Jason and Dave spun Shaun around and propelled him up the footpath with a solid shove in the back.

He collided with Spud who was on her way to see what was happening, and everyone around broke into giggles and cheers as, to avoid ending up on the ground, Spud clutched at Shaun and Shaun clutched at the chain-wire fence. With a scathing glare that somehow managed to take in the entire group while centring on her brother, Spud picked up her bag, seized Shaun by the arm and hustled him across the road.

They walked home together. Normally, Shaun

would have enjoyed the situation, but this was the second time in a week that his pride had been injured and Spud had witnessed them both. He need not have worried. If she noticed his burning ears, she made no comment. Instead, all she wanted to do was ask about Sam. Shaun filled in a few sketchy details, but was in no mood to talk, even to Spud.

Sam was not at the pizza hut. Shaun was partly annoyed that he hadn't shown up and partly worried that something might have happened to him. They waited for about fifteen minutes, but in the end Spud said she had to get home and she would catch up with him later.

Shaun wandered off towards the Walkers' place circling around the block so as not to run into Rick or any of the others. It occurred to him, though, that he couldn't avoid them forever. Sooner or later he would have to face them. Even if he was allowed back into the group, it would be a long time, if ever, before he rose above third-class status. There was little chance of that now; he had burned his bridges by challenging Rick.

Anyway, he began to realise he didn't want to go back. It was so long since he had felt free to be himself, he had almost forgotten who that person was. Now that he had remembered, he didn't want to lose himself again.

4

Disembodied voices

DEEP IN THOUGHT, SHAUN WAS ON HIS WAY down the path to his flat when Mrs Walker rapped on the kitchen window. Startled, he looked up and she beckoned. He didn't really want to talk to anyone just then but, now that she had caught his eye, he had no option but to climb the verandah steps to see what she wanted.

'Shaun, you've got a visitor,' she announced as he entered the kitchen. And there was Sam, sitting at the kitchen table, cake crumbs on the plate before him. Shaun was happy enough to see him, but determined to let him know how much trouble he had caused.

'How the hell did you get here?'

'Shaun!' Mrs Walker frowned. 'I don't like a guest spoken to like that.'

'Sorry, it's just that I told him to meet me at the Pizza Hut and he never turned up.'

'He had your address on a letter you sent him.' Mrs Walker indicated a creased and grubby envelope on the tablecloth. 'He got tired of wandering around Blackwood and knocked on the door about half-an-hour ago. So, now that you are both here, what say you introduce me?' Shaun was surprised that Mrs Walker had let Sam in the house if she didn't know who he was, but then she was like that.

'Didn't he say?'

Sam answered, 'I wanted to wait till you got home.' He looked down at the table, engrossed in picking up crumbs on the end of his finger and replacing them on the plate. 'You explain,' he mumbled.

Shaun related how they had met, thrown together against their will on the sheep station. He half-expected Sam to object as he told about Jack Dobson's drunken abuse of his family, but Sam said nothing. He told Mrs Walker about the overnight camping trip that had taken a dangerous turn, testing their courage and cementing their friendship.

'Sam's Dad got another job in Leigh Creek,' he said in conclusion. 'Sam stayed for the rest of the holidays, but then he went there to live with his family again and I came here to go to school.' Mrs Walker sat in silence for a minute, regarding the two boys in turn.

'Well now,' she said gently. 'Your mother must be worried, Sam. Would you like to ring her and let her know you're okay?'

'Phone's been off for a while now.'

'All right, does she have some friends who could pass on a message from you?'

'I suppose so, but I don't know their phone numbers or anything.'

Mrs Walker considered him thoughtfully for a moment. 'Sam,' she said, seating herself across from him at the table, 'would you mind if I prayed for you? Not here and now; later, on my own. One thing I've learned is that there is no situation so bad that good can't be squeezed out of it somehow.' Sam looked a bit embarrassed, but nodded.

'All right,' Mrs Walker continued. 'Now, how's this idea? I'll phone the minister at Leigh Creek and ask him to visit your mother. He can tell her you're safe and that you are welcome to stay with us for a few days until you decide what to do next.'

Sam thought about it before he answered. 'Okay, but don't tell him your address. If Dad. . .' He hesitated. 'If Dad finds out where I am, he'll come down and get me.'

So it was decided. Mrs Walker made the call, then set about cooking dinner while Shaun took Sam down to the granny flat and pulled the spare mattress out from under his bed. Mr Walker arrived home and seemed quite happy with the arrangement once it was explained to him; conversation at the table avoided sensitive subjects without seeming to try. Then, just as the boys were washing the dishes, the doorbell rang. Spud was ushered into the kitchen and explained shyly that she wanted Shaun to help her with some homework. She offered her Maths book as evidence, but nobody was really fooled. Mrs Walker relieved Sam of the tea-towel and shooed them all out the back door.

They talked. Eight o'clock came and went, then nine. There was an openness in it that Shaun didn't feel when he was with Rick and the others. He didn't have to pretend he was enjoying himself; he didn't have to watch what he said — or didn't say — or the way he said it, or the words he used in case he sounded like an idiot. And he didn't have to try and gauge which jokes to laugh at and which to ignore. They just talked.

Spud plied them with questions about the bush in general and Turtleshell in particular. She made them recount in detail the ordeal they had been through, nearly two years ago now, in the gorge at the north end of the property. It had been in the papers and on the news, but she had not realised Shaun was one of the two boys involved.

Shaun began the narration, but before long it was Sam who was telling much of the story. Spud was held entranced. Their struggle to right an old prospector's crashed vehicle and drive the injured man to safety had been played out against a backdrop of rugged beauty which Shaun saw again with new wonder as his friend described it.

Shaun told of his exhausting run through the

moonlight to radio for help from the other side of
the hills and Sam, after some prompting, told of the
fearful hours of waiting, freezing under the stars,
pretending to be asleep, not knowing when their
captors might check and find that he was alone.
Shaun discovered for the first time what had sus-
tained the Aboriginal boy through that dreadful
night: it was the knowledge that he was lying on
ground made sacred by 10,000 years of dreaming.

Spud was perched on the edge of Shaun's desk
next to the intercom and jumped when it squawked
right beside her. Shaun rolled off his bed and answered it. 'Shaun, is Spud still there? Her parents
will be getting worried.'

Spud leaned across and pushed the button. 'It's
okay, Mrs Walker, there's only my dad and he's
working late shifts this week.'

'Well, all the same,' came Mrs Walker's voice, 'you
and Shaun both have school tomorrow. How about
coming up to the house and I'll drive you home?'

Spud pulled a sour face at the intercom, but her
voice was sweet enough as she replied, 'Okay, I'll
be there in a few minutes.'

There was a click as Mrs Walker switched off, and
the next moment all three of them were staring at
the little speaker grille in amazement as a man's
voice, distant and disembodied, issued from the device: '. . .not just cops, though. There's security
patrols on the docks, there's customs, coastguard —
any number of things could go wrong.'

'Hey, settle down.' It was another voice now, deeper, rougher. 'I've done three of these trips without a single hitch. No sweat. The passengers are drugged, so they won't give you any trouble. There's nothing to worry about. If you keep calm, you'll be fine. Trust me.'

The friends stared at each other now. 'Who. . .' began Spud, but Shaun and Sam shushed her into silence as the first speaker continued.

'Trust you? That's how I got into this mess in the first place. I'll do it, of course. What choice do I have?'

'That's being sensible,' said the deeper voice. 'Now watch. You'll have to learn how to do this before tomorrow night. If we give them enough dope to last the whole trip it might kill them and they're not worth much dead, are they? So you'll have to top them up here before you take them to the boat. Let's see you use the needle on this little bloke.'

The conversation degenerated into grunts and disjointed comments and the three listeners bent their heads close to pick up the words. Their efforts were in vain, though, as several loud bursts of static masked the signal, then it cut out altogether. They stood around the desk, immobile for several seconds, eyebrows up, jaws down, before Spud finished her previous question. 'Who the heck was that?'

'No idea,' replied Shaun. 'Some sort of crossed line, I think. Yesterday I heard a woman talking on it.'

'Where are they?'

'I don't know. Not in the house, though.'

'Did you hear what they said?' Sam was grinning from ear to ear. 'They're kidnappers! They must be holding people for ransom. Like on TV.'

Spud was less enthusiastic. 'Sounded like they had children there. And he said something about a boat. Where do you reckon they would take them by boat?'

'Maybe they're selling them as slaves,' suggested Sam.

'Don't be stupid; they don't have slaves these days,' Shaun replied.

Spud frowned. 'Shouldn't we tell the police or something?'

'No way!' Sam was vehement. 'They wouldn't believe us anyway. What would you say? That we were listening in to someone's intercom and we heard them planning to drug children and sell them as slaves? They'd reckon we made it up.'

Shaun looked uncertainly at Spud. 'He's right, I guess. . .'

'Of course, I am,' interjected Sam. 'Cops never believe you, whatever you say.'

Spud still looked dubious. 'It did sound pretty unreal, didn't it? Like a spy story or something.'

'Maybe that's it,' said Shaun. 'We could be picking up a TV station. Perhaps what we heard was part of a movie.'

'Maybe. Even so. . .'

The intercom crackled suddenly into life and they all crowded around it again, but it was only Mrs Walker. 'Spud, I'm waiting. . .'

'Coming, Mrs Walker.' Spud said a hasty good-bye and remembered to collect the unopened Maths book on her way out the door.

The numbers on the bedside clock were fuzzy red blobs in the dark and Shaun struggled sleepily to pull them into focus. One twenty-seven. He groped backwards in his memory, trying to identify the sound that had woken him.

There it was again! The sharp rapping came from the window nearest the door. He sat up in bed and listened. Again the tapping, this time accompanied by a loud whisper: 'Shaun! Wake up! Let me in.'

He rose and opened the door a crack, intending to identify the caller first, but Spud slipped through the opening and shut the door behind her. Embarrassed, Shaun backed towards the closet to get a bathrobe to cover the jocks he habitually slept in, but he had forgotten the spare mattress and nearly tripped over it. Now Sam was awake and enquiring drowsily what was going on. Shaun and Spud tried to explain in simultaneous whispers and all was confusion for a moment until Shaun, clutching his bathrobe around him, found the switch on the desk lamp.

Sam seemed unconcerned as he sat up, took in the scene and grinned broadly. 'Interesting life you lead, Shaun,' he offered and, turning to Spud: 'Come here often?'

Spud was obviously agitated. 'Quick, get dressed, both of you. We've got to find those kids!'

'What kids?' asked Shaun yawning and rubbing his eyes. 'What are you talking about?' but Sam had caught on.

'The intercom. What those blokes were saying about drugging kids and taking them to a boat.'

'Oh, come off it. That was probably just a TV show, wasn't it? And anyway, even if it was true, how would you ever find them?'

'My dad's an electrical engineer,' answered Spud. 'When he got home, I asked him if it was possible to make those intercoms work between two houses. Told him Rick and I wanted to be able to talk to you whenever we liked.'

Shaun pulled a wry face. 'I don't think Rick wants to talk to me any more. So what did he say?'

'Well, apparently it would be possible if the two intercoms were tuned the same, but probably only over a short distance, like in the same street. He said it certainly wouldn't work between my house and yours even though we're only a couple of blocks away. He said stuff about transformers and, um, phases, but I didn't really understand it. The main thing is that it wouldn't work over a long distance.'

Shaun was still sceptical, but Sam was becoming excited. 'So if those voices were real,' he said, 'they're probably coming from a house within a block or two of here. That narrows it down a bit.' He looked at Spud in frank admiration.

The information was interesting, but Shaun still didn't understand how they could use it to unravel the mystery of the voices.

'Don't you see?' Spud explained. 'All we have to do is go along the street checking each house for, say, two blocks either side of this one.'

'What, you mean looking in windows and stuff?'

'Got a better idea?'

'Yes, go back to bed.'

Sam had grabbed his jeans and was wriggling into them under the blankets. 'Come on, Shaun, don't be a wimp.'

'But what if we get caught? We could wind up in gaol or something.'

Spud put a hand on his arm. 'We wouldn't really have to look in windows. We might find some clues in the yard or the garage.'

Shaun was still reluctant, but the pressure of her hand and the pleading look in her eyes overcame his caution. 'Okay, but we only look in yards.' He reached for his clothes, then hesitated awkwardly. Spud was gracious enough to turn her back while he dressed.

It had been raining. The road reflected orange street lamps in long, jagged stripes, and wet foliage hung heavy and low overhead. The light from Shaun's torch was almost lost, swallowed up in the cold, damp darkness. The sky was heavily overcast with only an occasional, ragged gap racing across the face of a watery moon. The three shadowy figures slipped surreptitiously along the street, standing in a nervous knot at the bottom of each driveway to debate whether the house it led to warranted investigation.

As they crept into the first yard, Shaun's limbs were trembling, whether from nerves or the cold he couldn't tell, and he was glad it was too dark for his companions to see him clearly. The garage had a locked roller door and apparently no windows so, after a whispered exchange, they moved carefully along the front of the house.

Blinds were drawn at all the windows and, at the corner of the house, a high, padlocked gate barred their access to the backyard. Sam was all for climbing the gate, but Shaun held him back. Still grasping Sam's elbow, he led the retreat back to the road.

'This is silly,' he hissed when they were safely off the property. 'How are we supposed to find out anything without breaking in — and I'm not going to do that!'

'I don't know,' came Spud's reply. 'We might spot something if they really are holding some kids prisoner. We have to try, don't we?'

'I know how to open locked doors with a credit card,' put in Sam. 'I saw a bloke do it on TV. You push it in between the. . .'

'For crying out loud! None of us has a credit card,' grated Shaun in exasperation, 'and even if we did, we're not going to be opening any locked doors. This is stupid!'

'Well, I'm going on, with you or without you.' Spud's determination came through even in her whispered declaration and, despite the darkness, Shaun could visualise her stubborn face. He sighed.

'All right. Let's do a few more, but only front yards. That's better than nothing, isn't it?'

They moved to the next property, but again there was nothing to be seen. Shaun persuaded them to skip the one after that, as he knew it was occupied by an old lady who went to Mrs Walker's prayer group. Even Sam had to concede that she was an unlikely suspect.

The next house was unoccupied. A sign on the front fence proclaimed that THIS DESIRABLE INVEST-MENT OPPORTUNITY was FOR SALE. The grimy windows were uncurtained and they were able to shine the torch into most of the rooms, but all they could see was a wooden chair and a few sheets of newspaper. There was no garage, only a carport which could obviously hide nothing. A small shed in the backyard was locked, but a torch-lit inspection through the louvre window revealed it to be packed almost solid with timber, rolls of carpet and tins of paint.

By the time the three entered the next property, they had become quite confident. Too confident. Shaun passed the torch beam over the garage door to confirm that it was padlocked and they stepped off the concrete driveway onto a gravel path. *Crunch!* It sounded like an explosion in a corn flakes factory! They all froze. Was the catastrophic crunch echoing around the hills or was it just his pounding heart? Shaun held his breath and strained his ears anxiously in the deafening silence. Nothing. They were safe. Carefully they moved onto the grass and advanced, parallel with the front of the house.

The dog was just standing there behind a wire fence, watching them. Shaun heard the rhythmic breathing and for a moment he could not identify the sound. Then, in the same sickening second that he recognised it for what it was, his eyes made sense of the dark shape behind the wire. Before he could do anything, the dog reared up, paws against the fence at a level with Shaun's head, and began to bark in a deep, guttural bellow.

Within seconds, a woman's voice could be heard in the room nearest to them and then the curtains glowed yellow as a light came on inside. Clutching his torch and pushing Spud along before him, Shaun headed for the road in a straight line across the front lawn and over the low brick wall. Sam tumbled onto the footpath behind them and Shaun thought he was in pain, until he realised that his friend's gasping was an attempt to stifle hysterical laughter.

'You should have seen you,' Sam choked as they lay in the wet weeds outside the wall. 'I swear your hair stood straight up like in a cartoon!'

'Didn't notice you standing around,' muttered

Shaun. Then, as the adrenaline drained from his bloodstream, he, too, collapsed into a fit of uncontrollable giggles. It was not until Spud tried to get up that Shaun realised his arm was wrapped tightly around her waist. She didn't seem to mind, though.

They held a council of war. The wind was rising and a fine rain had begun to fall, causing them to shiver and clutch their jackets around them. Also, the light from Shaun's torch, not brilliant from the outset, had faded to a feeble orange glow that lit nothing more than a metre away. They decided there was nothing to be gained by continuing. Before they parted, though, Spud extracted a promise from the boys to come out again the next night and try to finish the job. They couldn't just leave the poor children to their fate, she said. Shaun grunted his reluctant agreement and trudged back up the road.

Cold and fatigue conspired to erase from his mind the voices on the intercom. There were no captive children, of course, but there was little to lose and much to gain by humouring her. He tried hard to recall what his arm had felt like around Spud's waist, but he was too tired and wet and the memory eluded him.

Creeping back into the flat some time after two-thirty, the boys left their damp clothes piled on the floor and fell into their beds. Shaun awoke with a sore throat, running nose and sneezes. It took a little persuasion, but eventually Mrs Walker phoned the school to tell them he would be staying home.

5

The plan goes all wrong

SHAUN WAS DETERMINED to be better prepared second time around. He put new batteries in his torch and made sure both boys had warm clothes to wear. Their wet things had dried fairly successfully over the backs of chairs in front of a radiator and Shaun lent his guest a thick jumper while he got out a waterproof parka for himself.

Passing the time was no problem: though they had exchanged a couple of letters early on, they had not seen each other for over a year and there was a lot to catch up on. Shaun felt guilty about having ignored Sam when he turned up at the school, but Sam seemed content to let it pass without comment. In a funny sort of way, Sam's response made Shaun feel worse, as though he owed his friend a debt.

The two boys spent most of the day within earshot

of the intercom but, except for an enquiry from Mrs Walker about what they wanted for lunch, the device remained silent. They requested an extra sandwich each, but only ate a little, putting most of it aside to take with them.

Shaun still refused to believe in kidnapped children, but his sense of anticipation grew as the afternoon wore on. Partly, it was the thought of creeping into yards in the middle of the night, but at least some of it, he had to admit, was the idea of spending more time with Spud. For months, he had admired her from the safety of his association with Rick. Suddenly, though, in the space of two days, his friendship with this intriguing girl had moved to another level and he was prepared to risk a certain amount of discomfort to cultivate it.

They ate dinner as usual with the Walkers. In an effort to avoid giving away their plans for the night, Shaun and Sam talked overly loud and long about football and the weather, prompting Mr Walker to give them several suspicious, sideways looks, but they escaped without any direct questioning. Then they settled down for the long wait until eleven o'clock when Spud was due to arrive. There was a TV in Shaun's flat and they tried to watch a movie, but they were too wound up to pay it much attention.

Shaun had lain back against the pillows on his bed and was unaware he had fallen asleep until he felt

Sam's hand on his shoulder, shaking him. 'They're here,' he was saying.

After a moment's confusion, Shaun asked, 'They? What do you mean, "they"?'

'Spud's got someone with her.' Shaun was fully awake now. He sat up and rubbed his eyes, swinging his legs over the edge of the bed. Puzzled, he moved to the door and opened it. Rick! That was the last person he wanted to see. Spud preceded her brother into the room and, seeing Shaun's angry frown, spread her hands and shrugged apologetically. 'What could I do?' she said. 'He threatened to tell Dad if I didn't bring him.'

Rick pushed past her and confronted Shaun belligerently. 'Listen, I don't know what you and your Abo mate have got my sister into, but. . .' Sam took a step forward, fists clenched.

Shaun hesitated, not quite knowing whether to back Sam up against Rick or step between them to prevent a fight. He need not have worried; Rick faltered and blinked nervously, uncertainty replacing the aggressive set of his features. Perhaps this was the real Rick, thought Shaun, not so confident when faced with someone who wouldn't back down. Rick and Sam glared at each other for long seconds. It was Rick who looked away.

They were stuck with Rick, no matter what they thought. They tried to persuade him to go home, but he was moved by a brotherly concern for Spud, which Shaun had to admire. Sam, however, continued to glower at him whenever he spoke and gave him a wide berth as they got ready to leave, as though he had a contagious disease. So finally, after putting out the light and closing the door of the flat silently behind them, four shadowy forms crept up the drive, past the darkened house and into the street.

This time they turned left towards an area of winding roads and wooded slopes, with few street lights and fewer footpaths. The houses often nestled close to the back of the blocks, among tall eucalypts, with overgrown bush gardens in the front. This excursion felt different from the previous night, when they had surveyed the properties closer to the main road; those neat, flat lawns and concrete driveways seemed tame compared with what they faced this time.

To Shaun's surprise, however, the job was easier. It wasn't raining, for one thing, and a relatively cloudless sky revealed a nearly-full moon which lit their way adequately while casting impenetrable black shadows to hide in as they approached the first house. The driveway was unpaved, but still damp from last night's rain, so they made no noise as they advanced like army scouts from tree to tree. It was still cold, though, and Shaun was thankful for his warm parka.

The house was timber-framed, clad with weatherboard that badly needed repainting. The walls were thin and, as they huddled beneath the front window, they could hear the television clearly, a comedy with spasmodic canned laughter from the speaker and the occasional human guffaw from somewhere in the room.

The house stood on low stumps with horizontal slats attached to them. Shining the torch between the timbers, they could see the usual under-house junk: an old wheelbarrow, lengths of wood, a lawn-mower and a few small, unidentifiable shapes that could be anything.

Moving up the drive, past an old station wagon, they found a corrugated iron shed. The door was shut but not locked and, after a short debate, they decided to look inside. It was strangely disappointing. Another old car like the one in the drive stood in the middle of the earthen floor with the bonnet up and a cavity like an open grave where the engine should be.

As they stood around, flashing the torch beam into the dusty corners of the shed, revealing jars of washers, old tools and an upended kitchen chair, Shaun felt suddenly ashamed. They shouldn't be poking around in someone's life like this. 'Let's go,' he said, and led them outside.

The other three felt no such qualms. Even Rick was anticipating the next house with excitement. Shaun made a few lame attempts to dissuade them, but they were determined to go on and, although he didn't like the idea, he went with them.

The driveway that faced them next was wide and

surfaced with asphalt like a road. It swept up in a curve to a large shed which was half hidden behind the house. A light was on in the back of the shed, casting into silhouette a truck about the size of a small removals van. The rear door of the truck was open, but it was too dark to see what was inside. They moved forward in a bunch, motioning each other unnecessarily to be quiet.

As they neared the shed, Shaun became aware of a faint smell, familiar yet hard to place. He looked over at Sam and wrinkled his nose, shrugging. Sam flashed him a grin in the darkness. 'Fish,' he whispered and immediately Shaun recognised the scent.

They were about halfway up the drive, level with the house, when a wedge of light from an opening door leapt out across their path. Shrinking back into the bushes, they watched as two men emerged from the house, carrying between them a box a metre or so long. The men were talking and their conversation was clearly audible.

'Last one.'

'Good. I'm hungry.'

'You can eat later. You're already running late.'

The first man caught his foot on something and stumbled. The other cursed him viciously.

'Sorry! Nearly dropped it!'

'Better not, you idiot. We only get paid for the ones we deliver alive.'

Reaching the garage, the men slid the box into the back of the truck.

'Say what you like, I'm getting something to eat before I go,' declared the hungry one, walking back down the drive to the house. 'It's going to be a long, cold night.'

'Okay, but be quick about it,' growled the other, and followed him inside.

As the door closed and the shaft of light disappeared, the four friends looked at each other, half in shock, half in delight. Rick let out his pent-up breath in a quiet whistle. 'I didn't really believe all that stuff about kidnapped children. Thought you'd made it up.'

Spud's snub nose lifted in the air and her short hair quivered with indignation. 'Who'd make up a crazy story like that?' she said. Then, to Shaun's alarm, she broke cover and ran straight up the middle of the driveway towards the shed, bent double to avoid being seen from the house as she passed a window.

Shaun glanced at Rick, unsure of what to do. Spud reached the truck and, with one smooth motion, swung herself up onto the rear step and disappeared inside. Shaun's heart missed a beat as a shadow detached itself from the darkness beside the shed and glided silently across the lighted opening towards the truck. With a start, he realised that it was Sam. He had not even noticed the Aboriginal boy leave his side, so quietly had he moved. He glanced across at Rick and knew from his expression that he had seen the same thing.

Shaun grinned. 'Not bad is he?' he whispered, and jerked his head towards the truck. 'Come on, let's see what we've found.' Rick hesitated a second but, not to be outdone by the others, he followed Shaun up the driveway, hugging the shadows of the bushes.

As they reached the shed, they were met by Spud and Sam who had jumped back down from the truck. They huddled in the darkness between the open door and the fence as Spud reported. Her voice shook and her breath came in irregular gasps. 'There are three boxes in there, all the same. And guess what? They have lots of little holes drilled around the sides! Breathing holes!'

Shaun's heart pounded and his knees felt weak. 'Could you hear anything? See through the holes or something?'

'No. I knocked on the lid of one and whispered as loud as I dared, but they must be drugged. You heard what they said last night.'

'Police,' said Shaun. 'We have to call the police.'

'Ha!' barked Sam. 'Even if they believed us, the truck'll be gone before they get up off their —'

'He's right,' agreed Spud. 'Those men will be back any moment. They'll drive away and we won't know where they've gone.' In her excitement, she had raised her voice to an urgent hiss and Shaun looked anxiously towards the house as she contin-ued. 'This may be our only chance to rescue those kids. Listen, the tops of the boxes are held on with four screws. If we can get the kids out and screw the lids back on, those guys won't know they're gone till it's too late.'

Spud fitted action to her words. Slipping around the open door, she reached up and grabbed a screwdriver from a pegboard on the wall above a workbench before walking boldly to the back of the truck and climbing inside once more. Again Shaun hesitated, then, as he moved to follow her, Sam seized his arm and drew him back into the shadow of the shed. The house door had begun to swing open and the two men appeared, shrugging heavy coats on as they shut it behind them and walked rapidly up the drive to the truck. The three boys watched in horror as the larger of the two men swung the rear door of the truck closed with a thud that seemed to strike Shaun in the centre of his chest, interrupting his heartbeat. A long bolt was slid firmly home top and bottom, securing the door, and the two men stood facing each other in the lighted entrance of the shed.

'Time to go,' said the big man. 'Just relax and you'll be fine. Boat's at No.3 Dock; that right?'

'Yes. No.3 Dock. Look, are you sure you want to come? It's going to be pretty rough out there.'

'Too right. My, uh, clients have a big stake in this cargo. You leave without me and I can't guarantee your safety at the other end. Understand?'

'No, I don't. The weather report's bad. There's one hell of a low pressure system coming across the

Bight. If we don't make the rendezvous before it arrives and beat it back to port, I can't guarantee anyone's safety. You'd better not hold us up too long.'

'I've got a couple of loose ends to tie up, but I'll be there. You wait for me, you hear? Now get moving!' With that, he turned on his heel and strode down the driveway to the road. A car door opened and shut, an engine started and headlights flared as the car accelerated away up the hill.

At the top of the drive, the other man waited while the engine's sound faded into the distance. His features as he stood motionless by the truck were thrown into shadow by the light behind him, but Shaun guessed he was frowning. His brain raced. Maybe they could talk to him, explain. . . The man turned, flicked off the light in the shed and swung himself into the cab of the truck, slamming the door.

Suddenly, the paralysis that had gripped Shaun for the last few minutes was gone and he stood up. They had to tackle the man. It was now or never. He looked at the others and, after a moment's uncertainty, they stood beside him. But it was too late. The starter whined, the engine fired and the truck backed past them, gathering speed down the driveway. In his shock, Shaun's senses seemed suddenly sharper. The truck seemed to slide past in slow motion, and he noticed little things like scratches on the side, the name 'R.J. Collins' on the door, a refrigeration unit looking like an air conditioner above the roof of the cab. Then it was gone, receding down the driveway with Spud inside.

No longer caring what happened, Shaun ran out into the open and chased the vehicle, waving his arms. The driver, though, had his eyes fixed on his mirrors, concentrating on reversing the truck, and reached the road without seeing him. Shaun shouted, but the noise of the engine must have covered the sound of his voice. Rick and Sam caught up with him at the bottom of the driveway and they watched the red tail light vanish around a bend. Shaun's brain went numb and his stomach churned with horror.

It was a disaster. They had lost Spud. He should have. . . He could have. . . Shaun had no idea how he might have prevented what had happened, but he knew it had been up to him and he had failed.

Without warning, Rick whirled around towards Sam and grabbed a double handful of his jumper, shaking him violently and shouting, 'Now look what you've done!' After his initial surprise, Sam responded, lashing out at Rick's shins with his feet and hammering with his fists at Rick's stomach and ribs.

Shaun tried to intervene, shouting, 'Stop!' and 'What the hell are you doing?', but it was not until Sam managed to land a punch on Rick's nose that the brawl fell apart and Shaun was able to step between them.

'It's not Sam's fault,' Shaun told Rick as the taller boy panted and dabbed gingerly at his nose with a handkerchief. 'Spud was the one who. . .'

'Of course, it's his fault!' shouted Rick, pointing at Sam. 'Ever since your boong mate arrived, all she's been able to talk about. . .' Sam lunged at him again, and this time Shaun was in the middle of it. All three boys crashed to the ground in a heap, skinning elbows and knees on the rough road surface. Shaun was the first to untangle himself. Kneeling beside Rick, he tried to help him up, but the other boy knocked his hand aside angrily.

'Look,' said Shaun, 'it makes no difference whose fault it is. She's gone. We have to get her back. It's time to call the police.'

'No!'

Shaun straightened up and rounded on Sam. 'Listen, I don't give a damn what you think of the police; we need them now. Every minute we waste, she's getting further away. We have to call them.'

'No, listen. Please.' This time there was desperation in Sam's voice. 'If we get the police, they'll want to know who we are and what we were doing. They'll call our parents. My dad will come and take me home.' He stepped forward. In the light of a solitary street lamp, his dark eyes mirrored the pleading note in his voice. 'You know what he's like. I can't go back there.'

'He's right', said Rick.

Shaun turned and stared at Rick in disbelief. 'What?'

'Our parents will find out what we were doing. My dad will kill me.'

Shaun was getting angry. 'Who cares? Spud's in that truck. She's your sister, isn't she?'

Rick's eyes flashed with sudden fire and he raised a clenched fist. Shaun flinched, waiting for the blow, but Rick lowered his hand stiffly to his side. 'That's just what he'd say. With Mum gone now and him at work, Spud's my responsibility.' He screwed up his eyes and shook his head. 'He'll kill me,' he repeated.

Shaun's own father could be pretty awesome when it came to issues of right and wrong, but Shaun had never been afraid of him, and he didn't get drunk and bash him like Sam's dad. He looked from one earnest face to the other, trying to understand, but seeing no alternative. 'Look,' he said, 'none of us have done the right thing, not even Spud. We shouldn't even be here. If we had told the police in the first place, we wouldn't be in trouble and Spud wouldn't be in that truck. But it's done and now we can't change that. I can't see any other way to get her back.'

'We'll just have to,' stated Sam with determination, and Shaun nearly screamed in his frustration.

'Who do you think you are? Superman?'

Sam stepped closer. 'Look,' he said, 'we know they've taken her to No.3 Dock.'

'And you know where that is, I suppose,' returned Shaun, sarcastically.

'I grew up in the Port. Only been out in the country for a year or so.'

Shaun gave ground reluctantly. 'All right, but

where does that get us?' he asked. 'What can we do?'

'We get down to the Port as fast as we can and find that truck, or the boat they're loading the boxes onto. Soon as we know for sure where she is, we call the cops. You heard them; they have to wait for the big bloke before they sail, so we've still got time.'

Shaun looked at his watch and sighed. 'No, we haven't. The last train has gone. And anyway, it would have taken us over an hour to get down there. I still say we should tell somebody.'

'Taxi,' said Sam. 'Is there a phone box around here?'

'So we can change into our costumes?' said Shaun bitterly, but the others ignored him.

'There's one up at the shops,' answered Rick.

'Okay, then, let's go!' And, with that, Sam turned and began jogging up the hill towards the main road.

Rick followed Sam and soon caught up, leaving Shaun to follow reluctantly in their wake. Since this whole affair had started with the voice on the intercom, Shaun had felt sucked into things against his will. Every time he stopped to think about what they were doing he knew it was foolish, but the arguments of his friends and the momentum of the events had drawn him on. Now it was out of control. He fully intended to turn in at Walkers' gate, but when he got there he faltered. The thought of waking them and trying to explain what was going on, how they had snooped in people's yards and garages, how Spud had come to be whisked away in the back of a truck. . .

Besides, a picture had begun to form in his mind of a daring rescue. Hadn't he and Sam done this before? Last time it had been an old prospector in an overturned Land Rover; this time it was a teenage girl, a damsel in distress. His imagination presented him with an image of how Spud might express her undying gratitude as he swung open the door of the truck and snatched her from the jaws of fate. Yes, they could call the police after they found her, he thought, as he set off once again after Rick and Sam.

6

Hot pursuit

BY THE TIME SHAUN REACHED THE MAIN ROAD, the other two had crossed to the row of shops on the far side. They were standing under a light outside the snack bar, heads close together, apparently discussing something Rick held in his hand. Shaun was halfway across the road when the figure of a man emerged from a darkened door to their right, turning to lock it behind him. Seeing the two boys lurking outside the shop, the man took two strides towards them and placed a hand on the shoulder of each. Shaun heard Rick yelp in fright and saw Sam spin around with one arm raised in defence. He smiled to himself as he trotted across the last few metres to set things straight.

'Veg!' Shaun called. 'It's okay; they're friends of mine.'

The owner of the Gaslight Chicken shop turned at the sound of Shaun's voice and, recognising him, released his two nervous captives. 'You sure, Shaun?' he asked dubiously. 'Looked to me as though they were up to no good.'

Shaun introduced them. 'This is Sam; he's been staying with me for a few days. You probably know Rick; he just lives a few blocks away.'

Veg was still unconvinced. 'If you're not up to mischief, what are you doing here in the middle of the night? Shops are all shut; the only reason I'm still here is I had to fix that darn rotisserie again.'

It was Rick who came to the rescue. 'Well, you see, Sam has to get home. He was supposed to be back in Port Adelaide half-an-hour ago, but we lost track of time. Now the last train's gone. His dad's going to be really mad. We were going to call a taxi, but we don't have much money.' He held out his hand, revealing the change they had been counting. 'How far do you reckon he could get for $5.45?'

Shaun rummaged in his pocket. 'I've got two dollars,' he offered.

Veg sighed and rolled his eyes to the sky. 'Why me?' he asked. 'All right, but I'm still not sure I believe you.' Pulling a wallet from his hip pocket, he extracted a twenty-dollar note and handed it to Shaun. 'Here, take this. I want it back, okay?' With heartfelt thanks, the boys turned towards the telephone box at the end of the row of shops, but Veg called to them again. He picked up a white plastic shopping bag that he had left in the doorway and offered it to Sam. 'Here's a chicken for your dad.

Might keep him off your back. Be good!' he called over his shoulder as he walked to his car.

The taxi driver didn't believe them either, but he had been waiting at the rank by the post office for nearly an hour, he said, and he wasn't about to argue with a fare to the Port. He made them show him their money first, though, and seemed friendly enough once he knew they could pay. He didn't get much response to his attempts to make conversation as they wound their way down from the hills; there was not much the boys could say, even to each other, that would not have blown their story. Finally, he gave up and resorted to giving them the occasional curious look in the mirror.

The traffic was light, and they had soon skirted the city and were nearing the top of Port Road. As they passed the police barracks, a siren leapt into sudden life as a patrol car entered the road and passed them, lighting up the interior of the taxi with red and blue flashes. Shaun had been immersed in a restless sea of conflicting thoughts about their predicament and jumped guiltily. The eyes of the cab driver regarded him with interest.

Shaun settled back deeper into the seat and they swept on down the wide, empty highway towards Port Adelaide. Passing under the railway bridge, the cab slowed as they approached the centre of the town. Masts and derricks showed above the low warehouses ahead, illuminated by lights on the wharf. The streets were empty except for an old man who shuffled along the footpath with a potato sack, picking through garbage bins.

The driver's eyes appeared again in the mirror. 'Where to now?'

'Black Diamond Corner,' Sam answered with easy familiarity. 'Just here. Yeah, this'll do.'

'Sure?' The driver was obviously reluctant to drop three schoolboys in the middle of the Port at that desolate hour.

'My dad lives in the flat above that shop there,' lied Sam, pointing vaguely out the window. 'We'll be okay from here.'

Shaun paid the driver and they waited in the shadow of a verandah until the taxi had executed a U-turn and accelerated back towards the city, chasing a radio call. In the back of his mind Shaun knew that, even then, they could have found a phone box and called someone, but they didn't do it. Instead, they set off on a road that ran parallel to the waterfront, Sam leading, on their quest to rescue Spud. The three musketeers, thought Shaun. It seemed impossible that they should fail, as they strode purposefully along the deserted street, their steps echoing in a strangely thrilling syncopation from the darkened shopfronts.

Sam seemed to know where he was going. He explained that they were heading for a road which led out past the warehouses and rail yards to No.2 Dock and, beyond that, No.3 Dock where he had often fished for mullet and bream. Their spirits lifted and they drew confidence from each other. They walked side-by-side down the middle of the road, joking about what they would do to any driver who dared to run them over. They shared the chicken, sucking their greasy fingers noisily and eventually leaving the plastic bag full of bones hanging on someone's car aerial. Although they now had no doubt that their mission to release Spud from the truck would soon be completed, they kept the sandwiches they had salvaged from lunch until later. Just in case.

They turned left off the main street. An arm of the harbour extended almost back to the road they were now walking, with dilapidated wharves on each side. A railway track crossed their path at that point, and Shaun's eyes followed the line of rusty rails where they ran out along the dock beside deserted sheds. Light from a bank of blue-white arc lamps on the far side of the harbour threw the sheds into sharp relief and created black wedges of deep shadow that could conceal — well, anything. With dark, forbidding warehouses and dark, oily water, it all seemed suddenly menacing and the skin along Shaun's spine prickled. A pair of heavy boom gates barring access to the wharf were painted in diagonal black and white stripes as if to say, 'Go back, you should not be here.' The threatening atmosphere seemed to infect all three boys. They didn't joke any more, but continued on towards the next line of low buildings in silence.

It was No.3 Dock, Sam assured them, although Shaun could see no sign or other indication that he was right. Without realising it, the boys moved closer together as they approached. Two cranes, standing on tall, skeletal legs, faced each other, towering like monstrous insects guarding the dock. Shaun could feel them watching him from blank window-eyes high in the air. They were further now from the bright lights across the harbour and the shadows were thicker. A line of white mooring bollards that crouched at regular intervals along the edge of the quay stood out against the inky-black water like pale, misshapen creatures from another world. The moon had disappeared behind heavy clouds and the wind was rising, carrying the smell of rain, but that was not the reason Shaun shivered.

There was only one boat in the dock, a fishing vessel tied up near the end of the wharf on the far side of that stretch of black water. There were no lights visible aboard her, no signs of life. The boys looked uncertainly at each other, unwilling to make the next move.

'Can you see the truck?' Sam whispered.

'Not from here,' answered Shaun, 'but it might be. . .'

'Yes, look!' Rick pointed to where the boat was moored. Shaun saw nothing but darkened sheds. 'There,' insisted Rick. 'Between those two sheds. Right near the boat,' and with a quickening of his heartbeat, Shaun saw that he was right. What he had first taken for a lean-to extension of the second shed along the dock was actually the back of the truck, drawn up close to the wall in the gap between that shed and the last.

'Okay, let's go and have a look.'

'Yeah, let's go.' For long seconds nobody moved; then, keeping together, they skirted the end of the dock and hurried into the shadow of the first shed. As they huddled beside the corrugated iron wall, an icy wind, whipping across the harbour, sliced through the denim of Shaun's jeans. He was glad he had worn his parka. Glancing across at Sam and Rick, he saw them wrap their arms around their bodies and turn their faces away from the chilly blast.

Bent almost double, they made their way cautiously along the front of the shed until they came to a gap between that one and the next. They were close enough to see the boat quite clearly now. There was still no sign of movement from the vessel; only its own uneasy motion against its mooring lines, as though it was nervous about staying so long in such a place.

Scuttling across the patch of open ground like commandos, the boys paused again in the darkness on the other side. They listened. A sudden, iron clatter from the shed they crouched by made them jump, but it was only a heavy sliding door moving in the wind. One by one, Shaun identified other sounds: the whistle of wind in an electric wire, the slap of water against the side of the wharf. There was a soft, periodic groaning which puzzled him at first, but which he eventually equated with the motion of the boat against the side of the dock.

A single lamp on a post about halfway along the shed spilled an insipid pool of light down the rusted iron wall and onto the uneven ground at its foot. The only way to get around the illuminated area would be to venture out into the middle of the wharf and, as Shaun pointed out, that would take them perilously close to the boat. They could still see nobody aboard her, but that didn't mean she was deserted. Sam had the answer. If they ducked back around the other side of the shed, they could move up to the gap where the truck was parked and use its bulk to conceal them from the boat.

They turned and moved, still crouching, back around the corner of the shed. Pausing again, they stood up, stretching their cramped limbs. They were sheltered from the wind now, and the absence of its chilling effect immediately made them feel warmer. Out of sight of the fishing boat, they were able to walk upright instead of skulking like frightened animals, and this gave them back some of their confidence. Rounding the next corner, the boys advanced swiftly along the back of the shed to its far end. Sam, in the lead, peered cautiously around the edge of the building, then beckoned the others to join him.

The cab of the truck was only a couple of metres from where they stood. In unspoken agreement, they all moved forward together, stealthily approaching the vehicle until it loomed above them. There was clearly no-one in the front, but how were they going to approach the door in the rear without being seen? They were now directly opposite the boat, and anyone aboard would only have had to glance in their direction and it would have all been over. Rising on his toes and looking through the windscreen, Shaun could see that the refrigerated back of the truck was separate from the cab. No way through from the front, then. Moving around between the truck and the next shed, he saw to his delight that there was a side door to the truck as well as the one in the rear. He hissed to the others to come.

There was enough light to see that there was no padlock on the door. Reaching up, Rick gently turned the handle and pulled. There was a disappointing second when the door resisted his efforts and Shaun thought there must be another lock they had overlooked. Then, suddenly, it gave, swinging back with that sucking sound a fridge door makes with its plastic seal. It seemed loud enough to be heard on the other side of the harbour! They froze, Shaun with his eyes squeezed tightly shut, but there was no response from the boat; no shout of alarm, no light piercing the darkness, no running footsteps.

Crowding forward, the boys tried to see into the blackness, aware once again of the strong smell of fish. They whispered Spud's name, but there was no answer. Shaun pulled the torch from the pocket of his parka and risked a short flash around the inside of the truck, but his only reward was its reflection from the bare, stainless steel sides of the empty interior.

He switched off the torch and withdrew his head from the doorway, swinging the heavy door back into place. After only a few seconds of torchlight, the night seemed much darker. He could not make out the features of his companions clearly, but he could feel in them the same sense of deflation that was stealing over him. They should have been rescuing a grateful Spud at this point. It was not turning out anything like the heroic venture he had imagined.

Shaun led the retreat to the sheltered side of the shed, concern rising to panic in his chest, tightening his throat, making it hard to think straight. In the lee of the decaying structure, Rick leaned wearily against the wall before sliding down to squat with his back to the hard corrugated iron, his shoulders bowed in defeat. Sam squatted beside him and stared at the ground. Shaun, not quite knowing what else to do, placed a hand on Rick's shoulder and squeezed it gently. Rick's face, as he raised it to speak, bore two tiny, winking points of light on the cheeks, like diamonds, as two silent tears reflected lights from the next dock along. 'They've got her.' His voice was hoarse. 'They must have found her and taken her onto the boat. What are we going to do?'

Shaun had no answer to give, but closed his eyes

to avoid meeting Rick's stricken gaze. Standing there, with his hand on Rick's shoulder and his eyes shut, it suddenly seemed right to pray. Not out loud, more like reaching out in his mind for help. Strangely, he felt his own panic subside, like pent-up breath exhaled and, when he breathed in, it was with a sense of quiet confidence. Even the noise of the wind seemed for that moment to have abated.

He opened his eyes and saw that Rick was looking at him with a curious expression. Shaun smiled sheepishly and the answering smile surprised him with the unguarded honesty of its gratitude. Releasing his grip on Rick's shoulder, he shifted his gaze and was relieved to find that Sam's eyes were still firmly fixed on the ground between his feet.

Not for long, though. Sam suddenly looked up and answered the question Rick had asked in his despair. 'I'll tell you what we're going to do,' he declared. 'We're going onto that boat to find Spud.'

Shaun opened his mouth to protest. 'You've got to be crazy', he was about to say, or even, 'I told you we should've called the police.' But he hesitated and lost his chance. Rick leapt up, fully recharged it seemed, and extended his hand to Sam.

'Right. Let's go!' he agreed, hauling Sam to his feet, and once more Shaun was left trailing reluctantly behind.

The third shed, the outermost, lay at right angles to the other two, servicing the berths along the end of the dock. They had to move away from the truck, away from the boat, to get around it and, when they reached the end, Shaun wished fervently they could simply keep going. Back home. Back to bed, where he would wake in the morning and find it had all been a bad dream. But it was not, and soon they came to where they must double back around the shed, towards the boat.

The wind had not dropped; in fact, its strength seemed to have increased. Shaun could feel it buffeting him as he approached the end of the shed. It swirled around the corner, catching at his hair and raising gritty dust that stung his unprotected hands and crunched unpleasantly between his teeth. Rick and Sam had disappeared around the end of the building and Shaun peered around after them. It began to rain, a fine mist that was driven almost horizontally by the wind and found its way down the neck of his parka.

As he paused to raise the hood over his head and pull the drawstring tight around his face, the other two boys reached the next corner and crouched by it, waving at him to join them. He approached cautiously, although it occurred to him that, with the noise the wind was making, there was no way they could have been heard.

This corner of the shed was very close to the fishing boat. They were actually a bit further out along the dock than the vessel and, looking back, they could see it clearly in the feeble wash of light from the lamp that had first halted their progress.

It was smaller than Shaun had first thought, with the deck actually lower than the level of the wharf. But it was chunky and useful-looking, broad in the beam, with high, business-like bows to face the weather and a square, no-nonsense wheelhouse forward of centre.

On top of the wheelhouse, a short mast carried a radar aerial and, behind it, a complex maze of booms and cables, lifting gear for the trawl nets, swayed erratically. The only concession to appearances was the ornate lettering on the name board screwed to the side of the wheelhouse: *GINNY ANN*.

Ginny! The name spoken by the woman on the intercom. Shaun's heart beat faster.

7

No way of escape

IF THEY HAD SEEN THE WATCHER, they would never have risked the dash across the wharf to the boat. But they didn't; they squinted against the needles of rain and decided there was no-one on deck. Half-crouching again, they ran across the uneven surface, careful not to trip on the buckled steel of the old railway line, and made it to the shelter of a bollard. Its knobbly shape promised to disguise the outline of three heads as they huddled behind it and nervously surveyed the vessel.

If they had seen the watcher, they would never have dared to descend the rusty ladder that led down to a platform not far above the water. From there, a short, cleated gangplank rose and fell between the immovable edge of the dock and the restlessly swaying deck of the trawler.

Having come so far, though, even Shaun now felt committed. One by one they set foot gingerly on the narrow plank and stepped across. It was springy underfoot and, Shaun felt, decidedly unstable, but it only took a second or two and then he was standing on the deck. There was only room between the deckhouse and the rail to move in single file. Sam, closest to the stern, beckoned the other two in that direction and Shaun was glad to follow: if there was anybody aboard, he reasoned, they were more likely to be found further forward.

The first they saw of the watcher was the flare of a match in the darkness and the glowing orange reflection on his cupped hands as he applied the light to his cigarette. Rick sucked in his breath audibly and Sam swept his hand urgently backward as they flattened themselves against the superstructure. Shaun tried desperately to press his shoulder-blades into the cold steel behind him. He turned his head sideways, inching up onto his toes to see over Rick's head.

It was difficult to make out the silhouette of the man against the dark water, but he could see where he was by the glowing tip as he drew in the smoke. He was standing at the stern, looking back along the dock. They had been hidden from his view as long as they stayed by the sheds, the wharf being above his eye-level, but they would certainly have been spotted against the sky had they approached the trawler from the stern. Shaun's heart hammered home to him the stupidity of what they were doing.

He began to tug at Rick's sleeve. He leaned

forward until his mouth was close to Rick's ear and hissed, 'This is crazy! Let's get out of here while we still can!' Rick began to turn towards him and Shaun could sense his indecision. He tugged again. 'This really is a job for the police.'

Suddenly, Sam stiffened and pressed them back a second time against the side of the deckhouse. 'Too late!' he breathed, and jerked his head towards the edge of the wharf. Shaun's heart sank. There was a light shining on the narrow strip of wall they could see below the roof of the shed, a light which brightened, advancing along the underside of the rusty guttering as its source moved up the wharf towards them.

A car engine became audible through the bluster-ing wind and Shaun realised he could see the shocked expressions of his companions as the twin wedges of light, sparkling silver in the slanting rain, swung towards them. With sudden horror, he grasped what was happening: the driver of the car intended to park at the edge of the wharf with the headlights angled so as to illuminate the boat. An-other two seconds and the boys would be caught like rabbits in a spotlight!

Move! It was their only chance. *Go!* Shaun shoved Rick, who cannoned into Sam. *Get down!* He flung himself to his hands and knees and scram-bled towards the stern, pushing Rick roughly before him. As the car approached, the sharp-etched shadow of the edge of the wharf swept down the side of the deckhouse ahead of the brilliant blaze from the headlights. Sam and Rick realised the danger and crawled desperately along the narrow deck towards the sanctuary of deeper shadows. They were only metres from where the watcher stood, now clearly defined in the bright beam. Please God, let him be dazzled, let him not hear! *Go! Go!*

They were there! Sam rounded the end of the deckhouse and dived under a large steel table welded to the deck. Rick and Shaun bolted in after him and they cowered against a heap of damp nets, striving to control their heaving lungs. The space was crowded with baskets, plastic bins and coils of rope, but it was out of the path of that relentlessly swinging beam of light. Shaun's heart pounded in his throat until he thought he would be sick. The motion of the vessel as it rolled against the side of the dock, and an overpowering smell of rotting seaweed, added to his discomfort.

They were not a moment too soon. Footsteps sounded on the deck, passing them as the watcher left his post in the stern and went to meet the new arrival. They could hear a voice, raised in anger, challenging, pausing for a reply too faint to catch, then continuing. Shaun thought he recognised it as belonging to the man at the house, the one who had driven the truck. Some of his words carried above the noise of the wind and the slap of water on the hull. '. . .crazy . . .barometer's falling. . .' The words

were flung into the stormy night: '. . .maniac. . .
rendezvous in this weather. . .'

Shaun risked a look, crawling out a bit from under
the table. He could see the outer end of the gangplank and a large man in a thick coat standing at
its foot. He could not see him clearly as the car's
headlights were shining directly into his eyes, but he
thought it was the second man at the house.

The newcomer waved his arms to emphasise
words that could not be heard, then stepped forward.
He stopped as the other came into Shaun's field of
vision, moving out along the gangplank. They stood
in the wind-driven rain, arguing. Yes, it was definitely the pair who had loaded the truck. Spud *must*
be aboard, but where? And how were they going
to find her without being discovered themselves?

The man on the dock seemed to run out of patience. One hand went to the pocket of his coat and
he withdrew. . . what? Shaun could not be sure,
the night was dark and wet, but it seemed that
something in his hand gleamed in the headlights of
the car.

There were no more voices. Both men moved up
the gangplank until the corner of the deckhouse hid
them from sight. Had they gone inside? Shaun had
no way of knowing. Shadows swung wildly as the
car reversed, turned, and drove away down the wharf.
For about a minute, Shaun strained to catch any
sounds above the blustering of the wind. Nothing.

He beckoned to Rick and Sam and they crawled

out, one on each side of him. The three looked at each other and Sam shrugged. He stood up, cautiously, craning forward to see further around the deck. Suddenly, he whirled around and ducked back under the table, pulling the others with him. Heavy footfalls again sounded, along with faint shouts, and a dark shape moved past their hiding place, close enough to touch. A man was working on something near the stern, calling out as he passed them again on his way forward.

There was another sound that Shaun did not recognise at first, a deep whining, like an electric motor somewhere under their feet. It rose and fell rapidly for a few seconds until it was replaced with a rhythmic thumping. He knew *that* sound all right; he had grown up to the nightly beat of the heavy diesel motor that drove the generator at the homestead, but it was several seconds before the significance of it struck him. Then, oblivious to the danger of discovery, he again craned his neck and peered out from between the prawn bins. Yes, the dock was further away, the sheds sliding slowly backwards. Even as he looked, he saw faint flashes of light reflected from the widening strip of water between the boat and the wharf. They were under way!

Sitting together by the foul-smelling nets, the three boys held a desperate, whispered conversation. Shaun was close to panic again, and Rick to despair.

Sam's mood was one of tired resignation. 'Look,' he said with a sigh, 'maybe Spud escaped from the truck before they saw her, but I don't think so. Unless we jump over the side and swim, there's no way we can get off this boat until it gets where it's going, so we might as well carry on searching.'

'How?' asked Shaun. 'There are men on board. We'll be caught.'

'Big deal!' answered Rick. 'We'll be caught anyway when the sun rises. This isn't exactly a cruise liner! There's nowhere to hide once it gets light.'

'So, what do you want to do?' The scorn was obvious in Sam's voice, even though his face was in darkness. 'Do you want to just sit here and let it happen? She's your sister. Don't you want to find her?'

'What do *you* think? Of course I do, but then what?'

'How should I know?' hissed Sam. 'Maybe something will turn up. Maybe they'll pull into another dock, or at least get close enough to swim for it.'

'Sure, or maybe when they catch us they'll just say sorry and let us all go again.' Rick's voice was becoming louder now. 'I should never have let her come. I knew you couldn't be trusted, you. . .'

'Shut up, you idiots!' Shaun whispered hoarsely. 'They'll catch us right now if you don't keep your voices down.'

They sat in miserable silence for a moment, feeling the vibrating beat of the motor deep in the hull, until Rick spoke again. 'Look, I'm sorry,' he said. 'I'm just tired. And scared.'

'Me, too,' replied Shaun, 'and cold.'

'I don't know about you two,' said Sam, 'but I'm hungry. Who's got the sandwiches? Or did you eat them while we weren't looking?' Shaun smiled for the first time since they had reached the docks and fished in the pockets of his parka. The sandwiches were not too badly squashed and he divided them into three piles. Rick and Sam began wolfing their share down eagerly, but Shaun paused with a sandwich halfway to his mouth. His stomach was sending him conflicting messages. Although he was definitely hungry, he was becoming increasingly aware of the movement of the boat. It wasn't rolling exactly — more like a sort of slow corkscrew motion with a slight pause just before the end of each cycle.

He took a few deep breaths, possibly a mistake, considering the smell of the nets, and moved the sandwich a little closer to his mouth. It was no good; he couldn't do it. His final mistake was to rehearse it in his mind, imagining himself biting into the bread, chewing, swallowing. . .

'Here, you have it,' he said weakly, offering his portion to the other two boys. 'I'm not hungry after all.'

Their meal over, Sam and Rick obviously felt renewed, ready to continue their quest. Shaun just felt queasy, but stood up with them as they cautiously explored their surroundings. They were out in the middle of a long waterway with lights on each side slipping silently past. They could see dark mounds in some places. There were structures which Shaun recognised as silos and lower, wider shapes which Sam identified as petrol storage tanks. He assured them that they were heading down the Port River towards Outer Harbor and the open sea. Shaun expressed a hope that they might tie up at Outer Harbor, but he did not even convince himself.

Sam suddenly grunted as though making up his mind about something. 'Won't find her standing around here,' he said, and set off sternwards. Rick and Shaun looked at each other and then followed suit. Despite the rain and bitter chill, it was good to be moving again, no longer hiding in fear.

They skirted another sorting table like the one under which they had taken refuge, moving past some heavy winching gear and a square, covered hatch. Lashed to the deck at the stern they found a large inflatable boat with an outboard motor wrapped securely in canvas. 'Zodiac,' whispered Rick as they peered inside. Rounding the stern, they filed forward along the other side until they came to the deckhouse again. It was clear there was nowhere on the afterdeck Spud could have been hidden.

Sam stepped cautiously along the strip beside the deckhouse, sliding his hand along the rail to steady himself against the motion of the boat. With his heart beating hard, Shaun followed, with Rick coming along behind. Reaching a round-cornered window, Sam paused and edged his head around to see inside. Drawing back again, he shook his head, crouched, and advanced until he could straighten up on the other side. Shaun and Rick did the same. Next, he came to a sliding door. Turning back to the others, he asked what they thought about trying to open it. Too risky was the verdict. Better to search outside first. It would be nice to get in out of the wind and rain, though, thought Shaun. They moved on.

Shaun was finding it hard to maintain his grip on the rail. Partly it was because the water seemed to be rougher and the heaving of the boat greater, but mostly it was because his hands were so cold. Cold? They were freezing! His face, too. In the excitement, he had barely noticed that the misty drizzle had turned into genuine rain which soaked his jeans and sneakers and, chilled by the rising wind, threatened to turn his face and hands into ice blocks.

The deck seemed to slope upwards as they approached the bow; in fact, there was a place where they had to climb three steps to a higher level. They had reached the forward end of the deckhouse now and, turning the corner, they crouched with their backs against the bulkhead and surveyed the foredeck. There was not much of it, just room for another hatch cover between them and the bow. Shaun pointed to the hatch, raising enquiring eyebrows at the others, but Sam shook his head vigorously.

'We're right under the wheelhouse,' he whispered hoarsely. 'They'll see you.'

Sure enough, when Shaun took a cautious step away from the deckhouse and looked back, he could see the row of windows behind which somebody was surely at the helm, peering anxiously ahead as the boat butted doggedly up the dark, choppy waterway.

Lowering his gaze, Shaun took in the appearance of his two companions. Their hair hung in limp, bedraggled locks over their foreheads and their faces shone with water that ran down cheeks and dripped off noses and chins. Their clothes were soaked by now and they huddled, shivering, against the superstructure. The icy wind renewed its attack with fresh flurries of rain and the little vessel ducked and wove as though trying to avoid them. Shaun gasped as the squall cut through the sodden fabric of his jeans. Turning, he pressed his back once more against the deckhouse and crouched between the others.

No, he thought again, this was not at all how the rescue should be unfolding. There was a cold, wet world of difference between the romantic adventure of his imagination and the real thing. What idiots they were! Any time in the last two hours they could have pulled out. The Port wasn't that big and the trawler wasn't that fast; surely, the police could have found it. He shook his head, wondering how they had managed to convince themselves they could handle it alone.

Rick turned to him and his face looked ghastly, tinged with green by the starboard navigation light.

'Let's go inside and look. Let's get out of the rain.'

Shaun hesitated. 'They'll catch us.'

Rick was almost pleading now. 'I don't care. I'm freezing.' His lips were drawn back and he clenched his teeth to stop them chattering. Shaun looked at Sam, who returned a grim nod, and they moved on, rounding the next corner and completing their circuit of the boat.

8

Staring down the barrel of a gun

JUST FORWARD OF THE POINT where they had boarded from the gangplank, there was another door with a window set in it. Sam peered cautiously in, then gripped the handle. 'Here goes,' his eyes seemed to say as he glanced at Shaun before gingerly sliding it open. They slipped through one after another and the door grated closed behind them, shutting out the wind and rain. Their new surroundings seemed almost silent by comparison.

Huddled together, dripping and shivering, the three boys looked around them. Although Shaun was grateful to be off the exposed deck, he was acutely aware of the increased danger in which they had placed themselves. He felt as though they were in enemy territory now and reached out with all his faculties, listening, feeling, smelling, gathering in all the information his senses could bring him.

The first thing he noticed was the warmth. Partly, he supposed, that was in contrast to the increasing chill they had endured on deck. The deep, throbbing vibration of the engine, felt through the legs and stomach more than heard, was again apparent now that the blustering wind and hissing rain were reduced to a murmur. Then there was the smell; the scents of diesel fuel and oil reminded him strangely of home, but other odours, alien and unfamiliar, kept him on guard.

Looking around him, he saw that they were in a narrow corridor which ran from one side of the deckhouse to the other, lit by a single globe in a steel mesh cage on the ceiling. Two doors on their right, towards the bow, and two on the sternward side of the passageway, were all tightly shut. Which way to go? Shaun was relieved to see Sam move to the left: presumably at least one of the right-hand doors led to the wheelhouse and he certainly didn't want to go that way.

Sam opened one of the doors that led towards the stern and ducked though it. Shaun and Rick moved to follow him. They never got there. Footsteps rang on a metal ladder to their right, a door handle rattled and a huge, bearded man emerged, almost filling the narrow passage. Shaun had not seen this man before; he was taller than the two at the house and built like a bulldozer. The man froze, still gripping the door handle, and Shaun watched his bushy eyebrows creep up until they disappeared under the shaggy mane of his hair. His lips were invisible behind a heavy moustache, but they must have moved because a deep voice issued from them.

'Strike a light!' it rumbled and Shaun felt Rick flinch beside him. 'How many more of you are there?' Shaun's eyes flicked to the door on his left, but Sam had shut it. He stepped back involuntarily as the big man moved towards them, but there was no escape. One huge paw gripped his arm and the other captured Rick, then the hairy giant turned them, an awkward manoeuvre in the confined space, and propelled them through the door from which he had arrived. They were faced by a steep, iron ladder. 'Up!' was the command and the grip on their arms was released. Shaun glanced behind, but the exit was completely blocked by the bulk of their captor. 'Up!' he repeated. Shaun led Rick up the six steps into the wheelhouse.

There, in a square room with large windows on three sides, the motion of the vessel was more pronounced and Shaun had to keep a hand on the rail of the ladder where it emerged from the floor. The wheelhouse was in darkness, except for a faint glow from the instrument panel, and the man who sat in a tall chair at the helm was visible only as a dark shape against lights on the shore that dipped and swung with a disjointed rhythm.

Shaun moved aside to allow Rick to join him. A disk of glass in one of the windows spun rapidly with a whirring sound, forming a clear circle in the rain-lashed pane through which the helmsman peered intently. Perhaps it was that sound that masked their arrival, or perhaps he was absorbed in guiding the boat past buoys and channel markers; the man did not turn until the bearded crewman stepped into the wheelhouse and addressed him.

'Skipper.'

The skipper swivelled in his seat and looked in their direction. He seemed not to see the boys in the gloom until they were pushed forward where they could be dimly illuminated by the glow from the instruments. Shaun could not see the helmsman's face, but his voice registered frustration after the initial surprise.

'What. . . Oh, come on! Where the hell are they coming from? Crawling out of the bilges?'

A low chuckle escaped from deep inside the crewman and to Shaun the sound was strangely reassuring. 'I reckon someone's been selling tickets for this trip.' After that, even the expletive that burst from the helmsman's lips seemed less threatening than it might.

The skipper turned back to the wheel and steered in silence for a minute. When he spoke again, it was with weary resignation. 'What about Jacobson? Has he seen them? Does he know they're here?'

'No.'

'Good. The less he knows about this, the better for all of us. See if you can get them past him and into the locker with the girl.'

Shaun's heart leapt and he opened his mouth, but Rick beat him to it. 'Spud. She *is* here, then!'

The skipper turned his head again. 'Sure is, mate, under lock and key, like you will be until this trip is over. Now, get them out of the wheelhouse, Steve; I've got to concentrate.'

Once again, the crewman's iron hand encircled Shaun's arm and he and Rick found themselves stumbling awkwardly down the ladder. Somewhere in the background of his thoughts, Shaun's brain was still busy feeding him information. The skipper's voice was familiar to him. He was definitely one of the men they had overheard on the intercom (When? Last night? The night before? Shaun was exhausted and his sense of time was beginning to blur.) He was the driver, the one who had stood in the moonlight by the open shed after loading the boxes into the truck. Boxes! The kidnapped children! Shaun had become so absorbed with their efforts to rescue Spud, he had entirely forgotten what had set them on this crazy course in the first place.

Out in the passageway, they were shepherded towards the other door on the forward side. Suddenly, the one opposite it burst open and Sam spun out into the corridor, crashing painfully into the wall with his shoulder. The man who followed him through the door didn't see them at first; he had grabbed Sam by the collar and given him a teeth-rattling shake before he noticed the passage was not empty. He wore a heavy overcoat and Shaun was sure he was the one who had arrived by car, the one who had helped load the truck. The man's eyebrows shot up, then plunged down, almost meeting above his bulbous nose.

'More! Well, are they yours or did they blow in on the wind?' Behind Shaun, Steve made no reply, unless you counted the low growl that rumbled in his throat. 'Go and take the helm,' ordered Sam's captor. 'Tell Roy I want him here.'

The crewman hesitated, and Shaun could feel his anger through the hand on his arm. Deftly changing his grip on Sam, the passenger reached into the pocket of his overcoat, the same sinister movement he had made at the gangplank. Shaun had never seen a real pistol, but the object which menaced them now looked very convincing. The pressure on his arm was reluctantly released and, though he could not take his eyes off the little black hole in the snout of the weapon, he could hear the crewman's boots on the iron steps leading to the wheelhouse.

Dragging his gaze away from the gun, Shaun turned his attention to Sam. His left cheek was cut and a trickle of blood ran down to his chin. Despite the dark skin, the cheek was beginning to display a darker patch of bruising. His eyes were screwed up in pain as he massaged his shoulder. All at once, Shaun's weariness evaporated and a flush of anger surged through his chest. He slipped a glance at Rick and was shocked at the intensity of the fire which flashed in the deep-set eyes. A knot of muscle twitched at the side of Rick's jaw as he clenched his teeth, and for a second the face projected such fury that Shaun felt sure the man must see it and be warned.

Footsteps sounded behind them and the skipper's voice was sharp. 'Okay, Jacobson, what the hell's this about?'

'You tell me,' was the gruff reply. 'What say we all sit down and discuss it.' Jacobson motioned with the pistol and backed through the door, pulling Sam with him by the collar. Shaun, Rick and the skipper followed.

They found themselves in a small room with a table fixed to one wall, bench seats either side of it. Above the table was a window through which Shaun could see cranes, illuminated by bright lights, and the masts and superstructure of a ship lit up like a Christmas tree. The whole scene rose and fell steadily, and Shaun realised that he was becoming so accustomed to the motion of the boat that he had ceased to notice it. He also realised that he was very hungry.

Sam was pushed roughly into one of the seats, and the waving pistol indicated that Rick and Shaun should slide in beside him. The passenger seated himself across the table from them and laid the gun on the laminex surface. The skipper remained standing. Jacobson regarded each of the boys in turn. The flesh of his face was soft and round, with a nose like a blob of dough, but the eyes set like small, black pebbles above the plump cheeks were as hard and cold as steel. He applied his gaze to the skipper.

'Where did these kids come from, Roy?'

'I haven't got a clue,' replied the skipper. 'Perhaps they're undercover cops.' A tiny smile tweaked one corner of his lips, but it disappeared as Jacobson's eyes narrowed dangerously.

'Are there any more children on your vessel, Roy?'

The skipper hesitated before answering. 'As far as I know, just one.'

The other man lifted his right eyebrow. 'One more. And where is he?'

'*She* is in the chain locker. We found her in the truck when we came to transfer the cargo.'

The eyebrow came down to meet its partner, knitting the smooth, plump face into a vicious snarl. 'And you brought her aboard? You threatened this operation without consulting me?'

'Now you wait just a moment!' The skipper placed his hands on the table and leaned forward, belligerently. 'It might be your operation, and God knows how I let myself get sucked into it, but this is my boat. I say who comes aboard her and. . .' the tone of his voice hardened '. . .I say who goes ashore. I am the master of this vessel and you are a passenger. I think it's crazy trying to make a rendezvous in the dark in this weather — the barometer is falling like a rock — but for the money your people are paying me, I'll give it my best shot.

I hope you're a good sailor because, once we're outside the breakwater, it's going to get a lot rougher than this.'

Jacobson was not impressed. He merely touched the pistol gently, running his forefinger delicately up and down the smooth, dark barrel. 'All right. What do you propose to do with these kids? I reckon our best bet. . .'

'You can reckon whatever you like when you're ashore. On my boat, we play by my rules.'

Shaun flinched as the passenger's pudgy fingers wrapped around the butt of the pistol and lifted it off the table, but it was only to replace it in the pocket of his overcoat. 'Have it your own way, *Captain*.' He rose from the table and moved towards the door into the passage. As he opened it, he paused and turned his head, an unmistakable threat in his eyes and his voice. 'But if they give us any trouble, we start playing by *my* rules.'

The door closed and the skipper leaned once more on the table but this time, it seemed, with great weariness. His chin sank onto his chest, he closed his eyes, breathing deeply for several seconds, and Shaun suddenly felt sorry for him, sorry for the trouble they had caused and sorry for the unknown pain this man was bearing. It never occurred to him, or apparently to the other two boys, to do other than sit and wait until the skipper spoke. When he did, his voice was quiet, almost a whisper.

'Okay, what *are* you kids doing on my boat? I

tried to find out from the girl, but she acted like some kind of prisoner of war; wouldn't say a word.' Rick's eyes flashed again with fierce satisfaction and he almost smiled.

Sam spoke up. 'We know what you're doing. We know what you've got in those boxes; we overheard you.'

The skipper pursed his lips and narrowed his eyes thoughtfully. 'And what do I have in those boxes?'

Sam lowered his voice dramatically. 'Kidnapped children!' he breathed.

The skipper straightened up in surprise and it seemed for a moment that he was either about to laugh or cry. Then he passed his hand wearily across his eyes and composed himself. 'Well,' he muttered, as much to himself as to the boys, 'if I didn't have any kidnapped children aboard before, I damn well have now.'

He opened an overhead locker and pulled out three folded blankets which he threw on the table before the boys. 'Let's go,' he said brusquely, indicating the door with a jerk of his head. He shepherded them across the passage and through the door opposite, which revealed an iron ladder, the twin of the one leading to the wheelhouse, but angling steeply down into the belly of the vessel.

It was cold at the bottom of the ladder, and the iron walls seemed moist. On their left, the inside of the hull sloped in towards the floor and curved ahead of them, making the space narrower towards the bow. A low, iron door faced them, secured with a sliding bolt. Shaun was in the lead and the skipper ordered him to open it. He did, pulling the heavy door towards him. They were pushed through from behind, stumbling and tripping over unseen obstacles as the door clanged shut, plunging them into absolute darkness.

Shaun shuffled forward, catching his foot on some obstruction, falling against a pile of something rough, flat. Canvas. A tarpaulin. There was something else, cold and lumpy, under his knees. Chains. The others gasped and grunted and blundered against him as they tried to find their bearings. He stood up and red fire burst through the blackness behind his eyelids as he cracked his skull on the iron deckhead. The flaring colours in his brain faded though green and purple along with the sounds and sensations around him. He was toppling forward slowly, slowly, never reaching the canvas, but wondering why the smell of it made him smaller and smaller until at last he disappeared completely.

9

A fall

HE WAS BACK AT THE CAVE. *The sun beat down redly on the rugged cliff above the great black rock they called the Turtleshell. This time, the boy hanging by his finger-tips above the chasm was himself.*

They were all there, watching him. Sam and Rick leaned over the edge, grinning down on him and inviting him to come to the skate ramp; Jason, Dave and Nina stood further back, waving cheerfully. His mother looked up from the table where his father was carving an enormous chicken. She beckoned him to come and eat, frowning when she couldn't hear his reply. In fact, although people's lips were moving, the only sound Shaun could hear was the pounding of surf as the gale whipped the sea beneath him into a frenzy of foam-capped breakers. They rose higher and higher, now smashing against the sides of the gorge, now wetting his shoes.

His fingers were cold, numb, and he couldn't tell if they were still clutching the rock. They must be, or he would have fallen, but soon he must lose his grip. . . let go. . . His head ached. From somewhere behind him, his father's voice murmured, 'Stop and think first; you'll save yourself a lot of trouble that way.'

There was no time to stop and think, though. He had to find her. Where was she? Not in the cave. Perhaps she was in the sea that raged and fumed at his feet. He should go and look. He opened his fingers and saw himself fall from the lip of the cave, a huge, foaming swell of sea water rising up to engulf him. The world turned watery green as he sank down to the rocky floor of the gorge. Dry grass and bluebush swayed rhythmically in time with the surging of the waves above, and Shaun looked anxiously about him as he swam the length of the gorge, searching for Spud. Old Joseph, the prospector in the back of his overturned Land Rover, had not seen her. Neither had Dave the station hand who came riding up on his motorbike, slapping dust off his hat as he paused to chat about next month's shearing.

Then Shaun heard her voice, faintly, calling to him from above. He was nearly out of breath. His lungs burned and his heart thumped harder and harder as he struggled upwards, guided by the sound of his name. 'Shaun, up,' she was saying. 'Up. Up.' He didn't know if he could make it to the surface before the urge to open his mouth and suck in water overwhelmed him. He could see a light flickering through the wrinkled surface of the sea above him. It grew brighter as the voice in his head became more insistent. 'Shaun, Shaun. Up.'

He burst through the boundary of the water, into a

world of raucous sounds and chaotic motion. Mountain-
ous waves lifted him into the dark sky, roaring like a
blowtorch, before dropping away beneath him in a sicken-
ing swoop. He hit the bottom with a booming vibration
that seemed to reverberate through the room for ages before
it died away and the sea rushed him upwards again. All
the while, that dazzling light shone in his eyes, making
his head pound, and Spud's voice went on and on.
'Shaun, Shaun. Wake up, Shaun.'

He opened his eyes in the darkness of the Ginny Ann's
chain locker, rolled onto his side and vomited.

10

Locked up in the darkness

SHAUN FELT GHASTLY. His head ached unbearably. Every time he tried to sit up, it shot barbs of pain down his neck and into his shoulders, making him feel sick again. The world was a bedlam of noise and bewildering motion. As the three boys were bundled into the locker, the *Ginny Ann* had passed beyond the protecting arm of the breakwater and pushed out into gale-driven swells that crowded up St Vincent's Gulf from the south-west. Where the friends crouched, in the very prow of the vessel, the heaving and pounding of the steel hull and the crash and swish of the seas were fearfully magnified.

Every few seconds, the little boat would bury her nose into the flank of a wave and a foaming tide would hiss across the deck above them and roar in the scuppers as she struggled upward, shedding water under her rails. Reaching the crest at last, she would hesitate, as though afraid, before toppling forward, plunging into the next trough, bottoming with a gut-wrenching jolt that sent a deep quiver rebounding the length of her keel.

The darkness in the cramped compartment was complete, for they had decided to conserve the torch batteries for emergencies. They had only been used twice since the boys' capture: once in anxious attempts to revive Shaun and once in order to explore the chain locker. It was clear, though, that the only way out other than the door they had come in by was a square hatch in the ceiling. Undoubtedly it was the one the boys had seen from above; it was low enough to reach easily, but all their attempts to move it were futile. Just as well, really, Sam observed: if they did open it, the waves would rush in and quickly swamp them.

Darkness, Shaun discovered, tended to heighten his sense of smell, a regrettable fact, since he was not the only one in that confined space to have succumbed to nausea as the *Ginny Ann* bucked and twisted on her course down the Gulf. Spud had spread one of the blankets over him. Now, he rolled himself up in it, as much for comfort as for warmth.

That was the only bright point in the dark misery that had begun to settle over him: at last, they had found Spud. Shaun lay and listened as the others quizzed her. The conditions in their tiny prison were not the best for conversation, and Rick and Sam were inclined to interrupt with questions and comments, but she was eventually able to tell her story.

After climbing into the truck carrying the screwdriver, Spud had attacked one of the screws on the nearest box. She had just begun, when she heard footsteps on the drive, and was barely able to drop flat behind the box before the driver reached the truck. By the time she realised what he was about to do, it was too late; the door swung shut and she found herself in darkness. She considered shouting or banging on the side of the truck, but if these men were really kidnappers, she reasoned, they would have no hesitation in adding her to their cargo. Besides, she had the screwdriver. If she stayed in the truck and managed to free the children, perhaps they could all escape together later on.

The engine started and the truck backed down the drive. Spud lay between two boxes, clutching the screwdriver, until the steadier motion indicated they were up on the main road, then she set to work. It was a long job removing the first lid. She had to feel for the screw heads with her fingertips, guide the blade of the screwdriver into place by touch, then hold it there with one hand while she turned it with the other.

Of course, she could not see where the truck was going, so every bend in the road and every stop-start at an intersection was unexpected, throwing her off balance and, more often than not, jolting the screwdriver out of its slot. However, she directed her full concentration to the task, glad of something to take her mind off the inky blackness around her and the possibilities she must face at the end of the journey.

One by one, the screws came away, and Spud put them into the pocket of her jacket for safekeeping. She had an idea that if she reattached the lids to the empty boxes, even though they would be lighter, they would appear undisturbed and that fact might buy her time to escape.

Eventually, all four screws were in her pocket and the lid could be removed. She squatted by the box for a long time, staring towards it, straining to penetrate the blanket of darkness that surrounded her, wishing there was some alternative to what she was about to do. The long, narrow box was just like a coffin and somehow, with the screws removed, she felt strangely vulnerable, no longer protected from whatever lay inside.

From somewhere in the back of her mind arose dark, fearsome shapes, half-formed thoughts that made her hands shake and her stomach turn to jelly. Every horror movie she had ever watched, every ghost story she had ever heard, provided images which struggled to arise from her memory and present themselves to her cringing imagination. She tried to push them back where they had come from, but with no picture of the real world before her eyes to distract her, the ghouls of her own mind crowded in and threatened to overcome her.

She began to shake uncontrollably, then to cry.

The truck lurched around a corner and she fell sideways between the boxes. It was all too hard. It wasn't fair. She had not cried since her mother's funeral, and eight months of being strong and doing without her came rushing out in the flood of tears.

At this point in Spud's story, as Shaun realised what a grim time she must have had, first in the truck, then in the darkness of the chain locker, he began to wish he could comfort her. He heard a rustle of clothing and imagined Rick putting a brotherly arm around her. However, when Sam gently prompted her to go on, and she continued, their two voices seemed to come from very close together.

Spud had cried herself out and, being Spud, got herself back to the job. The release of emotion had banished the ghosts, it seemed, and she was able to make herself lift one side of the lid and slide it gently off. The strange, rank odour which wafted from the open box almost unravelled her fragile self-control again, but something vaguely familiar about the smell urged her on. Or perhaps it was just that she had no alternative. She reached out her hand in the darkness, desperately wanting to know what was in the box, but earnestly dreading what she might find.

'Feathers?' Shaun was the first to find his voice, though his brain still didn't understand what it could possibly mean.

'Yes, feathers. At first I thought it was part of some clothing, a fur coat or something, but that was only for an instant. As I moved my hand a bit, I could feel the wooden partitions inside the box. Each. . .'

Rick interrupted her. 'Hang on a minute. Are you saying there *wasn't* a kid in the box? '

'Oh, no. Didn't I tell you that at the beginning? No, it's birds.'

'*Birds!*' Rick's voice was incredulous and Shaun could almost see the astonishment in his face. 'Birds? Do you mean we've been through all this. . .'

'Hey, let her finish!' This time it was Sam who interjected, but Rick was beginning to get angry.

'You made me think you had discovered some kind of kidnapping racket. Oh, you idiots! I thought these guys were crooks! Now, we've followed them all this way, sneaked onto their boat. . .'

'Oh, shut up, Rick!' Now, Spud had waded into the argument. 'Of course, they're crooks. We knew that right from the start, when we heard them talking on the intercom about police and security patrols, remember? And anyway, people who aren't crooks don't lock kids in poky little holes and sail out into storms with them.'

Shaun felt it was time he came to Spud's aid. He didn't want all the support to come from Sam: she might get too grateful. 'Yes,' he said, 'and there was that guy with the gun.'

Spud had not heard the boys' story yet and was alarmed at talk of a gun. They filled her in briefly, then pressed her to go on with her account.

The box, she said, was divided into about twenty rectangles by a cross-hatching of wooden partitions. Each compartment contained a bird with its wings and feet confined by rubber bands. They seemed to be dead, as they didn't move when she stirred them gently, but she hoped it was just because they were drugged. Once she knew they were birds, she recognised the smell: her next-door neighbour kept budgies and she had occasionally been allowed into the aviary to see the eggs lying in their nest-boxes.

Although Spud was relieved not to find a child in the box, she became more bewildered the more she thought about it. Squatting by the open box in the darkness, she struggled in her mind for answers. A terrible thought struck her: suppose the men who loaded this truck were not those they had heard on the intercom at all? She didn't know what would be worse: to be discovered in the back of the truck by crooks, or to be found by perfectly innocent bird-lovers and have to explain her presence.

But surely, she thought, bird-lovers didn't transport their stock like this. And she was sure the voices were the same.

Then she remembered a program on TV about bird smuggling. Perhaps, that was it. The more she thought about it, the more fragments of memory fell into place. People overseas paid high prices for some native Australian birds, but it was illegal to take them out of the country. Something like that. She recalled images of birds packed in suitcases, in pockets sewn into the linings of overcoats — even in cardboard mailing tubes.

Well, there was little time left to wonder, for the truck swung sharply left, then right, then pulled to a halt. The engine died and the door of the cab slammed. Desperately, Spud felt her way to the front of the dark space, as far away from the rear door as she could get. She cowered in the corner, making herself as small and inconspicuous as she could. Maybe, if the light outside was poor, she could escape notice.

She heard a voice calling, then the bolt rattled and the rear door swung open. The darkness outside was punctuated with points of bright light reflecting off slick surfaces. She could see dark silhouettes of two men, one considerably bulkier than the other, looming in the open doorway. One reached to his left, a switch clicked and the back of the truck was flooded with light from a globe in the roof.

'Light?'

'You mean. . .'

Had he been able to see Spud's face, Shaun was sure it would have been turning bright red. Her voice certainly conveyed her embarrassment. 'Well, yes, it would have been a lot easier if I knew the switch was there, but I didn't, did I?'

'Okay. So the light came on. What happened? They saw you, I suppose?'

'Yes. I tried to bolt out past them, but the big one with the beard grabbed me. They could see the box was open and that I had found the birds. I struggled and yelled a bit, but he just put his hand over my mouth while they talked about what to do with me. I felt a bit sorry for them, really. They didn't want to bring me with them, but they couldn't take the risk that I would ring the police before they got away. When they locked me in here, they even apologised. I was pretty scared; well, I'd just spent half-an-hour in that dark truck, hadn't I? The big one came back with some food and a torch and a blanket. He said I was safer in here and that they would let me go when they finished the trip.'

Rick's tone was a little gentler than when he had last spoken. 'So, they *are* crooks, then. Bird smugglers. Well, are we heading for another country or what?'

'Another country,' said Sam. 'The way we're going, I don't think we will even make it out of the Gulf.'

It was true. Now that Spud had finished telling her story, they noticed the pitching and rolling of the boat again. If anything, it was worse than before. The little craft was rising and falling like a roller-coaster, and to the din of the storm outside was added an undertone of creaking and groaning from the fabric of the vessel herself.

Shaun had been thinking. 'I don't reckon we're going very far,' he ventured. 'The skipper was talking about a rendezvous. I think they're planning to meet up with another ship and transfer the boxes. I don't know how they're going to manage that in this storm, though. I can see why he was worried.'

Rick's voice sounded grim. 'We should be worried, too,' he said. 'You heard that Jacobson bloke. I can't see him letting us go to call the cops, even after the job is finished.'

'We could promise not to,' offered Spud.

'You think he's going to take the chance? You haven't met him; believe me, he doesn't look like the trusting type.'

They lapsed into silence for several minutes, listening to the storm and trying to convince themselves that the wild motion of the boat, as it rushed to the summit of each mountain of water and crashed into each valley, was not worse than before. Shaun still had a headache which throbbed with each shuddering drop of the hull and, when he gingerly explored the tender spot with his fingertips, he found the hair all glued together with dry blood. He wrapped himself tighter in the blanket, rolled over and closed his eyes, trying not to think of the pain in his head and the squeamish sensation in his stomach.

Shaun might have slept. If he had, he had no recollection of any dreams. He was roused by a hand on his arm, shaking him gently, and he opened his eyes to see the chain locker dimly lit by a torch which Spud held while Rick unwrapped a packet of sandwiches. On the canvas next to the food, there was a shiny cylinder which, when the torch light moved across it, turned out to be a large vacuum flask. Shaun felt a little dizzy, unable to compensate for the violent reeling of the boat, and Sam had to help him sit up. Huddled in their blankets, they gathered closely around the pool of light as though around a camp fire. Shaun was confused.

'What's happening? Where did the food come from?'

'The man was here again,' answered Rick. 'The one with the beard. He brought some hot soup as well. Said he was sorry he had to keep us locked up, but it was for our own good.'

'Hah!' barked Sam. 'That's a good one! He should be a cop.'

Shaun thought about that as he chewed his sandwich and sipped at the soup when it was his turn to use the cup. It had been Sam's constant refrain since the whole misadventure began.

'What is it with you and the police?' he asked. 'What's wrong with them?'

Immediately, Sam seemed to close himself off, as though an invisible curtain had been drawn between them. 'Forget it,' he muttered.

'No,' urged Rick. 'Tell us. We'd like to know. I admit it, we should have called the cops before we got into this mess. They would have done the job properly.'

'Yeah. Well, you're white, aren't you?'

'So what?' Shaun protested. 'They helped rescue you at Turtleshell when we got caught by those guys.'

'Course they did. Who do you think called them? Your dad. Different matter if it's a Nunga in trouble.' He looked at them one by one, dark eyes glittering fiercely below his unruly mop of black hair. 'You don't know what it's like.'

It was Spud who leaned across the circle and placed a hand gently on Sam's knee, searching his face and seeing in it the pain and anger that Shaun knew was never far from the surface. 'No, we don't,' she said. 'Tell us.'

There was a long silence. 'My cousin,' Sam began at last, 'the son of that uncle I came to see, he was down from Port Augusta. He had a few drinks, fair enough, but he wasn't drunk. It was late, and he was trying to get a room for the night in a hotel, but everyone said they were full. Didn't want a black sleeping in their beds, more like it. He had to take a leak, but he didn't want to go back into any of the pubs, so he went down an alley. Well, someone followed him and rolled him.'

'Rolled him?' asked Shaun. 'What do you mean?'

'Bashed him and robbed him. He needed that money for his bus ticket home. They hit him on the head with a lump of wood, but he staggered back into the street and waved down a police patrol. Big mistake. They arrested him for being drunk. Said he had alcohol on his breath and couldn't walk straight. While they were shoving him in the back of the paddy-wagon, one of them got on the radio

and said to get the cage ready. They'd caught another boong, he said.'

Shaun's cheeks burned and he lowered his eyes.
The word didn't sound funny when Sam said it.
'How do you know all this?' he asked.

'I was with him,' said Sam. 'I saw it. I heard it.'

Spud must have guessed there was more to the
story. 'What happened after that?' she prompted,
gently.

'They took him to the police station and put him
in a cell. For his own good, they said. The next
morning, when they went to get him out, they found
him dead. Hanged from the bars by his shoelaces.'

There was a shocked silence. Finally, Rick said,
'That's awful, but you can't blame the cops. He must
have been a bit crazy to hang himself like that.'

Sam's eyes bored into him across the circle. 'You
really *don't* understand, do you? He wasn't the sort
to kill himself. He had a job on a station outside
Port Augusta; he had a wife and two kids. What
would he want to kill himself for?'

Sam lowered his head, shaking it slowly in bewil-
derment. 'There was an inquest. They decided he
was drunk and also depressed from being robbed
and locked up. Said the bruises on his legs and
body were from the bashing he got when he was
robbed, but that's not true. He just got hit on the
head.' His shaggy hair shook again and, pulling the
blanket higher around his shoulders, he refused to
talk about it any more.

11

A life-threatening error

THE CHAIN LOCKER WAS IN darkness again. They had no way of knowing how long they were going to be shut in there, so they had agreed not to use the torches unless they had to. The cold seemed to reach out to them from the curved steel walls, sapping their strength and gnawing at their confidence. They rolled themselves in the blankets and lay close together on the rough canvas. Even so, with the light off, each one felt alone, preoccupied with their own thoughts.

The boat still leaped and plunged as madly as ever, leaning over to the left alarmingly as the wind strengthened further, but Shaun barely noticed it: his mind was on the story about Sam's cousin. Somehow, he had imagined that things like that only happened on TV or in other countries.

It was as though Sam inhabited another world from his, one where the everyday experiences of life were completely unlike his own. Anger, violence and death seemed to be a normal part of the picture Sam saw when he looked around him. The world Shaun knew was quite different. Apart from his grandfather, who had been very old, Shaun had never actually known anyone who had died, and only once had he been hit in anger — by Sam, before they both came to the city.

He had never given the police much thought, but he had always supposed they were the 'good guys': friendly, reliable and all the rest of it. The Walkers' neighbour over the back fence was in the police force. He sometimes waved cheerily to Shaun while he mowed his lawn and Shaun had occasionally seen him, looking tall and sturdy in his uniform, waiting for the train with other commuters. Surely, only crooks had to fear the police. And yet Sam seemed to have reason to hate them.

Maybe Sam was exaggerating. Or maybe his cousin's case was just an isolated incident. Or maybe not. Shaun struggled to understand how both worlds could exist together. He considered himself to be a firm ally of Sam's and yet (his face still burned at the memory) he had joined in the jokes along with his friends to impress them. When he was afraid of being left out of the group, forces too strong to resist had sucked him along, making him do things he would never have done on his own.

Maybe adults were the same. Perhaps even the pleasant family man over the back fence was capable of doing terrible things to preserve the admiration of his mates. It was a frightening thought and Shaun deliberately forced his mind away from it, onto other things.

His clothes were still damp. He was becoming acutely aware of how cold it was in their steel cell, despite the blanket, and he thought back to his warm, comfortable bed in the granny flat behind the Walkers' house. That led him to think of his own bedroom at home on Turtleshell Station. A sense of emptiness overtook him and he found himself reaching out again, as he had on Rick's behalf on the wharf, but this time for himself.

'Our Father in heaven. . .' There was a soothing familiarity about the words, bringing back in an instant the touch of his mother's hand and the sweet, lanolin scent of sheep on the breeze that stirred the curtains by his pillow.

'Hallowed be your name. . .' He was sitting once again on his father's knee in the firelight, leaning his head against his chest, feeling it rise and fall, listening to the beat of his heart and the amplified rumble of his voice.

'Your kingdom come. . .' He caught his breath. He had thought he was whispering the words inaudibly, but another voice had joined in, just heard above the cacophony of wind and water.

He was surprised that he felt no awkwardness as

he and Spud finished the prayer in unison. He felt the blackness deep inside him disappear, expelled by the lightness welling up from deeper still like the cool water that bubbled from the ground at Matthews Soak.

More voices than two said 'Amen' at the end and, in the silence that followed, he felt that a bond had been forged between the four of them that would see them through anything they might have to face.

The motion of the boat felt different. The little trawler seemed to have difficulty climbing the largest of the swells and sometimes they broke over her bows, roaring across the foredeck and smashing against the front of the deckhouse with an impact that could be felt through the entire vessel. It became necessary to brace your feet against the inside of the hull to prevent being tossed around inside the tiny compartment.

Shaun heard tinkling glass as the vacuum flask crashed against the door of their prison. Sam swore as the heap of chains shifted and a heavy iron link struck him on the shin. Someone vomited noisily and soon the stench that filled their steel cell made Shaun's own stomach heave and cramp.

Shaun felt cold, sick and thoroughly miserable. He did not begin to grow afraid, though, until he noticed cold water dripping on his neck. How long it had been going on, he didn't know; he only became aware of it when some ran into his mouth and the saltiness of it rang an alarm bell somewhere deep in his brain. He sat up.

'We're leaking!'

'What?'

'We've sprung a leak! There's sea water coming in from somewhere!'

There were anxious noises from the others as they untangled themselves from the blankets and sat up. Then the two torches flicked on almost simultaneously and began sweeping over the walls and ceiling, searching for the source of the dripping. It was the hatch cover. It was still firmly secured, but a welded seam along one side had opened slightly, leaving a crack where water trickled through whenever a wave rushed across the deck above. Even as they watched, the pounding sea opened the crack to the width of a pencil and the stream of cold sea water pouring through was enough to wet them all and set them gasping with cold and fright.

'You're right!' shrieked Spud. 'We'll be drowned if that cover comes off!'

Rick scrambled across to the door and began pounding on it with his fists. He had barely opened his mouth to shout, however, when the bolt rattled, the door swung open and he nearly fell through the opening. The bright light which spilled into the locker was dazzling, making them blink and rub their eyes. Visible against it was a dark figure which ducked under the low door and flashed a torch at them.

'Hurry!' It was the skipper's voice, edged with urgency. 'Get yourselves out of there and follow me!'

Crawling awkwardly out into the curving passage and standing up stiffly, the four of them shouted over the top of each other: 'What's going on?' 'Are we sinking? 'What's happening?' 'Do you know the hatch is leaking?'

The last comment caused the skipper to push past them and shine his torch back into the dark locker. He withdrew his head, his lips pressed into a grim line. Bolting the door, he hustled the children along the passage.

Shaun found it hard to keep his balance: he hadn't stood upright for hours and the violent pitching of the boat threw him repeatedly against the walls as he made his way towards the foot of the ladder. Once at the top, they congregated in the room with the table, and the skipper flung open the cupboard that had contained the blankets. Hauling out orange life jackets, he thrust them into the children's hands.

'Put them on. Quickly.'

'We *are* sinking, then.'

'I hope not, but I want you kids with me in the wheelhouse.'

'I have to go to the toilet,' groaned Sam, and Shaun realised he did, too.

'Tough luck! Hang on or do it in your pants. You'll be a lot wetter than that if I can't get us into Edithburgh in the next half-an-hour.'

He checked the fastenings of their life jackets and hustled them unceremoniously out into the corridor and up the ladder that led to the wheelhouse. The life jacket was bulky and uncomfortable, and Shaun wasn't sure whether to be glad to have it on or scared that he might have to use it. It made climbing the ladder awkward, especially as the wild swinging of the boat became more pronounced the higher he got, but before long they were all standing in the wheelhouse.

The light was very dim, but they could see Steve, the bearded crewman, at the helm, his enormous body obscuring much of the view. Not that there was a lot to see: it was so dark outside that Shaun wondered how it was possible to know where they were going. Jacobson's dark bulk loomed beside Steve in the half light and it was clear that they were in the middle of an argument. The skipper shepherded the four friends over to a corner of the room and told them to stay put. It was only a rail running around the wall at waist height that enabled them to stay on their feet. Jacobson turned at the sound of the skipper's voice and intercepted him as he made his way across to the helm.

'Why have we changed course?' he demanded.

'You still here?' replied the skipper. 'I was hoping you'd fallen overboard.'

'Shut your face, Collins,' snarled Jacobson. 'Just get us back on course and make that rendezvous.'

Shaun sensed the skipper was smiling. 'Whatever

you say, boss; this is your party. Just tell us where the spot is from here and we'll take you there.'

'What are you talking about?'

'Take a look outside! We could pass within twenty metres of them and not see them, or miss them by twenty kilometres.'

'Or get run down by them before we knew they were there.' Steve's deep voice startled Jacobson and he jerked around to face him.

'So where are we going?' he asked, almost petulantly.

'Edithburgh,' answered the skipper. 'If we can find it. It's sheltered there; we'll be just one more fishing boat riding out the storm.'

'If you can find it?' echoed Jacobson, a hint of fear overlying the anger. 'What about your radar?'

The skipper laughed harshly. 'Radar? Take a look for yourself.' He indicated the small glowing screen. 'Nothing but rain squalls and sea clutter.'

'For crying out loud!' Jacobson exploded, 'This is the twentieth century! Surely with all that technology. . .' He waved an arm at the array of instruments around the helm.

The skipper swung around to confront him, his face fixed with a kind of fierce joy. 'This is the sea, mate! She doesn't give a damn what century it is. Sure, there's a RACON beacon on Troubridge Island, but it's a funny thing, you know; the moment we invented radar, the sea came up with a thing called low pressure diffraction. In a depression this deep, we probably won't pick up the signal until we're aground.'

He stepped forward and Jacobson stepped back. 'Of course, we used to have Adelaide Radio until some Canberra bureaucrat decided it would be cheaper to base it all in Melbourne where we can't receive it in conditions like this when we most need it.' He turned away with a muttered comment that might have included an expletive and took up his station behind Steve.

Jacobson seemed to have run out of steam; he retreated to the safety of the grab-rail and clung to it. For several minutes, there was no movement in the wheelhouse except for the swaying of the skipper's body as he adjusted his balance to the wild motion of the boat, and no sound except for the howling of the wind, the hiss and crash of the waves and the whirring of that spinning disk of glass in the windowpane.

Eventually, though, the skipper leaned forward and peered at the instrument panel before moving to one of the rain-lashed windows on his left. He cupped his hands around his face and pressed it to the glass, remaining there for a long time before straightening his back. Then, he moved behind the helmsman's tall chair and repeated the performance on the other side. Stepping over to his crewman, he bent his head and they conferred in a low murmur. The bearded man nodded and swung the wheel, bringing the vessel's bows round to the left of her previous course.

From then on, the skipper seemed unable to keep still. Despite the lurching of the floor, he paced from one side to the other, occasionally pausing to cup his hands and peer out into the night. Perhaps it was Shaun's imagination, but it seemed that the windowpanes were not as opaque as before. They now showed as faintly lighter rectangles against the dark interior of the wheelhouse.

Shaun caught a movement out of the corner of his eye and turned to see Spud leave the stability of the wall and reel out across the floor, eventually clutching the back of the helmsman's chair. 'Can we help?' she asked. 'What are we looking for?' The men must have forgotten the children were there. Their heads snapped around in surprise and Jacobson advanced towards her with a snarl. The skipper stepped between them, staring him down. Jacobson's hand moved towards his coat pocket, hesitated and then relaxed. He shrugged and lurched back to the grab-rail on the wall. Satisfied that the moment had passed, the skipper turned to Spud and addressed her.

'Just a light,' he said. 'There's a lighthouse off the coast near Edithburgh, on Troubridge Island. It'll look like a tiny spark in the distance. If you see it, point it out to Steve and me. We have to keep the light to port as we approach or we'll pile ourselves up on Marion Reef.'

Spud nodded and moved to one of the windows.

Rick looked at the others and followed her example. They all left their corner and stationed themselves at various places around the wheelhouse, faces pressed to the cold glass.

Shaun felt a lightening of his heart now that they had something to do. Funny how things work out, he thought. These men had kidnapped them, locked them in a dark hole for hours and taken them out to sea in the middle of a storm, but now they were all cooperating to save the vessel and, perhaps, each other's lives.

Shaun had never been afraid of *death*; it was *dying* that filled him with dread: it might hurt and he had never been good with pain. He shivered as he imagined what it would be like to be sucked down into the cold depths, salty water flooding into his lungs. He was so deep in thought that for a while he forgot to look for the light.

It was Sam who saw it. 'There!' he whooped and leaped back from the window, pointing. The skipper stepped to the glass and peered out, cupped hands shielding his eyes from the instrument lights. Shaun stared in the direction of Sam's outstretched finger, but could see nothing. The skipper stood motionless at the window for nearly a minute. Suddenly, he straightened, grunted and slapped Sam on the back. He called a course correction to Steve, who swung the helm over again. Then, Shaun saw it, a tiny pinpoint of light off to the left, instantly extinguished. His spirits soared and he laughed out loud with relief.

As the *Ginny Ann* rolled and surged through the punishing seas, they all kept their eyes glued on the spot. The point of light appeared marginally closer each time they caught sight of it. The skipper divided his time between the instruments and the window, checking and rechecking the bearing of the light. After a while, he turned back from the window with a puzzled frown on his face. He looked again at the instruments, then circled the wheelhouse, peering through each pane in turn. Returning to the port side, he stared again at the spark of light, now visible for seconds at a time.

Suddenly, his breath hissed in his teeth and he whirled round with a look of horror. 'Starboard! Hard over, Steve! It's the wrong flaming light! Can you feel it? We're on the shoal!'

The helmsman spun the wheel desperately and slammed the throttle lever forward. The boat heeled over as her bows came around. Shaun could indeed feel a change in the rhythm of the waves; they were shorter, higher, with sharper rises and more violent drops than before.

As the bows swung further, Steve suddenly let go of the wheel with one hand and pointed. 'There it is! That's Troubridge!' He swore foully. 'We're in the red sector. We're over the reef all right!'

Sure enough, another light, higher in the air than the one they had been tracking, flashed ahead of them like a tiny, bright ruby. It flashed again, further to the left as they came about, and Shaun watched it, mesmerised, hardly knowing what to feel.

'Come on, come on,' muttered the skipper. 'Come around. Nearly there.'

Shaun clutched the frame of the window to steady himself and silently urged the little boat on as she clawed her way back towards the open sea. The first crash as she hit the bottom threw him against the window and, as he slid to the floor, he could taste blood in his mouth. The second shock flung him across the floor and into the wall. He could hear Spud screaming, and in that moment he knew he was going to die.

12

A life raft in a heavy sea

THE FLOOR WAS TILTED SO STEEPLY that Shaun could not move. He tried to stand up, but the bulky life jacket hampered his efforts and his feet just slid out from under him. The grinding and screaming of metal on rock carried through the walls and floor, filling the air with a ringing vibration that threatened to paralyse his mind. The vessel seemed to float free for a moment, struggling to right herself, and Shaun made it to his feet, clawing at the rail for balance. In the next instant, he was thrown violently back into the angle of the floor and wall as she hit bottom again with an agonised shriek.

Looking around in the faint grey light that now filtered in from outside, he gasped at the scene of chaos. Rick and Sam were trapped like himself against the wall, piled together in a tangle of arms and legs. The skipper was on his feet, clutching the grab-rail, shaking his head as if to clear it, and Jacobson lay crumpled in the far corner, motionless. Shaun was momentarily alarmed when he could not find Spud, but then he saw her, safely encircled by the enormous left arm of Steve who seemed riveted to the helm.

As suddenly as they had hit, they were clear. The grinding vibrations ceased and the vessel slowly regained a more even keel. One by one, they staggered to their feet — even Jacobson, who wiped his nose on his sleeve and stared with anger at the patch of blood it left.

Steve, at the helm, cursed loudly and spun the wheel. 'Trouble, Skipper! We've lost the rudder! Screw's damaged, too, by the feel of it. Or the shaft.' He reached for the throttle lever and pulled it right back. Shaun had grown so used to the monotonous thumping of the engine that for hours he hadn't even noticed it. Now its absence was frightening, making the noise of the storm seem louder and more menacing.

'Mayday! Mayday! Mayday!' Jacobson spun around as he heard the skipper, leaped across the width of the wheelhouse and struck the microphone from his hand.

As if by magic, the pistol appeared, waving inches from the skipper's face. 'Radio silence, remember?' he snarled.

The skipper stared at him in disbelief. 'You're

mad!' he gasped. 'Don't you know what's happening? We've got no steerage way. We'd be lucky if the hull's still intact; we're probably taking water! And we have kids aboard.'

'Whose fault's that? We've got a valuable cargo aboard, too, and I'm going to deliver it. The only calls from this radio are going to be mine.' He reached into his pocket with his left hand and produced a crumpled piece of paper. 'Get me this frequency.'

The skipper ignored it and stooped to retrieve the microphone. Shaun gasped as Jacobson's arm lashed out, the pistol barrel striking the skipper across the cheek, knocking him to the floor. Steve uttered a deep growl and rose from the high chair, but the gun swung his way and he sank back, glowering like a thundercloud. The skipper staggered to his feet, using the instrument panel for support, and touched his injured face gingerly. He shook his head and muttered, 'You're crazy!', but took the paper which Jacobson offered him once again. The boat still rose and fell, but her motion now was noticeably sluggish.

The radio was at one end of the instrument panel, a cluster of dials and digital displays. Pausing in front of it, the skipper turned again to Jacobson. 'Okay,' he said, 'I'll make the call, but at least let Steve get the kids off in the Zodiac.'

Jacobson's belligerent attitude faltered for a second. 'You really think we're going down?'

The skipper paused, feeling the movement of the *Ginny Ann* as she wallowed heavily in a trough and made hard work of rising to the next crest. 'Possibly. The wind's taking us past Troubridge and out into the Gulf. They might be able to get ashore on the island if they leave now, but in fifteen minutes it'll be too late.'

Jacobson was sweating now and the barrel of the pistol began to waver. 'Look,' urged the skipper, pressing home his advantage, 'you can tell your people where we are. If they want the cargo that much, let them come and get it. And us. If push comes to shove and we have to abandon ship, there's a standard inflatable life raft on the roof.'

Suddenly, Jacobson seemed to make up his mind. The pistol came up again and his voice was once more harsh and domineering. 'All right,' he said, turning to Steve, 'get the brats onto the island if you can. Me and the brave captain will stick with the boat.'

Steve looked at the skipper who nodded grimly. Sliding from the chair, Steve beckoned to the four and shepherded them towards the ladder. They were tired, and the boat was by now rolling drunkenly. Shaun slipped on the iron treads and was only saved from a nasty fall by Steve's beefy hand clutching his collar from above. Once in the passage that ran the width of the deckhouse, Steve fumbled with the fastenings on their life-jackets, checking and tightening them. The light was out, but a cold, damp greyness entered through the glass panel in the doors at each end of the corridor. It was enough for Shaun to make out the faces of his friends; they looked terrible, with pale skin and dark smudges under their eyes.

Steve moved to one of the doors and slid it open. Immediately the passageway was filled with the roaring of wind and water. Salt spray hissed past Steve and Shaun shivered as the cold air burst upon them. Steve hung onto the door frame for support and turned his face back towards them. 'Stay put!' he roared, but his voice was almost drowned by the noise of the storm. As he bent his head and thrust his bulk through the doorway, a dark flood rose above the edge of the deck, smashing against the superstructure, swirling around his knees and washing into the passage. Applying both hands to the door handle, he pulled the door closed against the weight of the water and was gone.

Shaun looked around him in the semi-darkness. How the heck had they come to be in this mess? What had he been thinking of? Some madcap idea of outwitting criminals like they had done on Turtleshell? But he had been on his home ground there, and the crooks had been on unfamiliar territory. Of course, there had been the romantic notion of rescuing kidnapped children. Hah! Children? He had put them all in danger, maybe even killed them and — for what? Three boxes of budgies, or whatever they were; he hadn't even seen the birds.

He was startled by a hand on his shoulder. It was Rick. He was saying something, but the storm was too loud and Shaun couldn't make it out.

'What?'

'I'm sorry!' shouted Rick.

'What for?'

'For not stopping you. I'm the oldest; I should have stopped you.'

The four were huddled together against the wall, heads close together. Spud looked up with a twisted smile. 'Don't kid yourself, big brother. You haven't been able to stop me doing what I want since the day I fell in the creek, remember?' From his grimace, it was obvious that Rick remembered.

Sam turned to Shaun. 'I hope your Mrs Walker *is* praying for me,' he said. 'It's going to take a miracle or two to squeeze any good out of this, don't you reckon?'

Suddenly, the door crashed open again and they staggered in shock from the fury of the elements that rushed into the narrow passage. Bracing his enormous body in the doorway, Steve bellowed at them to come. He was soaked from head to foot. His hair was plastered flat to his head and his beard whipped in the wind that howled over the sea.

He had a length of rope with him which he looped around their waists, knotting it with quick, expert flicks of his wrists and fingers. They must be frozen, thought Shaun. The end he tied around his own body before stepping back outside and ushering them through the door. As Shaun reached the door, the storm was punctuated by a loud crash. It might have been thunder, but it seemed to come from the wheelhouse above them. Steve heard it, too, and his head jerked upwards. He hesitated, then grimly went back to the task of transferring the children from the doorway to the dubious safety of the rail.

Out on the deck, the ferocity of the storm was horrifying. It no longer seemed to be raining, but it might as well have been. Although they were on the leeward side of the boat, solid sheets of spray swept horizontally along the deck and in seconds they were all wet to the skin. Even here, the wind pummelled their bodies and tugged at their clothes as they made their way along the rail towards the stern.

The little vessel rolled heavily, now lifting them into the howling sky, now plunging them down in terrifying swoops, until the mountainous waves rising on one side and the superstructure heeling over on the other seemed about to meet above their heads. Each time the rail dipped down, breathtakingly cold, foaming water surged up and over the gunwale, swamping them nearly to the waist. Then, as the *Ginny Ann* rolled back the other way, the flood cascaded back over the side, sucking and dragging at their legs as though reluctant to let them go.

It was only a few metres to the place near the stern where Steve had secured the Zodiac alongside, but Shaun wondered if they were going to make it.

Twice in that distance he lost his footing and clung to the rail, feet scrabbling desperately for a grip on the slippery deck. Eventually, however, they were there, and Shaun's mouth fell open in shock when he realised what Steve was asking them to do.

The Zodiac was inflatable, about three metres long, with an outboard motor clamped to the transom at the stern. Tethered beside the *Ginny Ann*, it rode up and down on each wave, sometimes a metre below the level of the deck and sometimes almost as high as their heads. Shaun could see no way they could board it without injury and his stomach knotted up with fear.

There was no rail here, and Steve stood at the edge of the deck above the roiling water, shaking out plenty of slack in the rope that attached him to the children. Gauging the relative movements, he stepped nimbly into the Zodiac as it passed him on the way down, stumbling only a little as he landed. Then he turned, braced his knees against the rubber side of the little craft and beckoned to Spud to follow him.

Spud looked grimly around at the others before stepping out across the gap towards the crewman's powerful hands. It looked easy. He simply reached out, gripped her by the waist as she jumped, and swung her safely into the bows. Then he turned back for Sam. As the raft swept upwards and the boat plunged down to meet it, Sam launched himself into the air, knocking Steve sprawling onto his back against the other side of the Zodiac. They sorted themselves out with some difficulty and then it was Shaun's turn.

The Zodiac rose. He waited until it came back down, but he was too slow and lost his chance. He teetered as he leaned outwards, thinking he might make the jump as it passed him on the way back up, but it approached with such terrifying speed that he chickened out at the critical moment. The Zodiac reached the top of the wave and began to fall again as the *Ginny Ann* rose. He plucked up his courage and screwed his eyes tightly shut. Steve wasn't going to wait any longer; the rope around Shaun's waist was yanked tight and he yelped, half in pain and half in fright as he tumbled out into space.

The next moment he felt strong hands around his arms and he was deposited in a dripping, freezing heap in about ten centimetres of water that sloshed back and forth over the bottom boards. He didn't care; he was just thankful to be sitting in the Zodiac and not swimming in the raging ocean.

Seconds later, Rick joined him in the raft and Shaun heard an explosive roar as the outboard motor burst into life. Steve scrambled over them, leaned across the soft rubber and began hacking with a knife at the rope that joined the Zodiac to the *Ginny Ann*.

'Hey!' yelled Rick. 'I reckon we ought to wait for them.'

'I agree,' returned Steve. 'Long as we can, anyway.

Safer if we stand off, though.' He clambered back to the stern, seized the throttle, gunned the motor and swung the Zodiac away from the trawler. No longer under its shelter, they were at the mercy of the wind again and Shaun wrapped his arms tightly around himself, clenching his teeth to prevent them from chattering.

Steve turned the Zodiac back into the wind, bow towards the *Ginny Ann*, and manipulated the throttle to keep them at a distance of about twenty metres from her. The tiny rubber craft twisted and bent as it rode over the huge swells, and the gale tore the tops off the waves and threw them in Shaun's face, but he felt surprisingly secure. Perhaps, it was the reassuring bulk of the seaman in the stern, or the sense that the flexible little boat was cooperating with the sea instead of fighting against it. Or, perhaps, he was just too exhausted to care any more.

Every time they reached the crest of a wave, he got a glimpse of the boat that had brought them across the Gulf. The sky was definitely lighter, though closed in with a ceiling of low, racing cloud, and in the dismal grey dawn it was clear that the *Ginny Ann* was sinking. She lay low in the water, broadside-on to the seas, dipping her scuppers under with every sluggish roll. The afterdeck was awash and the masts and booms swung tiredly through a wide arc.

Suddenly, the door in the deckhouse slid open and a figure was visible, waving to them. Steve twisted the throttle and, with a snarl from the outboard motor, the Zodiac began to close on the dying boat.

As they approached, Shaun could see the skipper (for the figure was clearly too tall and thin to be Jacobson) standing knee-deep at times in water, leaning against the deckhouse, fumbling with a box of some sort. Tucking it under one arm, he held something high with his other hand. Shaun thought for a moment it was Jacobson's pistol, especially when there was a flash and a puff of smoke from the object. A streak of light shot into the sky from the cylinder in the skipper's hand and exploded into a brilliant star high in the air.

'Got a flare off,' roared Steve. 'Good man!'

The flare sank towards the heaving sea, leaving a trail of smoke that the wind quickly tore to shreds, and Shaun was awed by the savage picture it revealed. The light winked and twinkled off waves, throwing the *Ginny Ann* into harsh relief against the dark water. In its stark illumination, Shaun saw the door in the deckhouse open once more and Jacobson burst out onto the deck, slipping and staggering in his efforts to keep his balance on the wet, heaving surface. He was waving the gun and shouting. Clutching the door frame with one hand, he brought the pistol up to shoulder level.

It all happened at once, but every detail was burned into Shaun's memory by the naked brilliance of the flare. As the Zodiac struck the side of the fishing boat, Steve let out a bellow of rage. The skipper's head twisted around and, seeing Jacobson's gun levelled at him, he hurled himself to the deck, the box falling from his grasp, scattering flares which rolled across the steel. The skipper struggled to his feet. Jacobson, moving surprisingly quickly for his bulk, scrambled along the rail until he came level with the Zodiac.

Jacobson's eyes were wild and he nearly spat with fury as he levelled the pistol and screamed at them. 'Get back! I told you to take those kids ashore. Now do it!' Swinging the gun towards the skipper, he stumbled forward, locating rolling flares with his feet and kicking them over the side. 'Try that again and you're dead!'

Steve threw the motor into reverse and began to back away from the trawler. The scene abruptly darkened as the flare reached the water and was extinguished, and Shaun realised with surprise that the entire event had taken no more than twenty seconds.

Swinging the Zodiac around in a circle, Steve set a course for the winking light, leaving the *Ginny Ann* behind. The fierce growling and muttering he kept up was a fair indication of his state of mind. Rick sat opposite Shaun, staring back over the stern as the trawler fell behind them, while Sam and Spud crouched in the bows. Spud's face was buried in Sam's sodden jumper and her shoulders convulsed with her sobbing. Although Sam was facing Shaun, his head was down and Shaun could not read his expression.

Over Sam's left shoulder, Shaun could see the lighthouse on Troubridge Island. It was definitely morning now and the tower was clearly discernible, standing above some dark, square bulk that could be a house. The light flashed white about once every ten seconds. If only they had been able to see it so clearly an hour ago. . . He realised that the wind was not as strong as it had been and, while the waves still tossed the rubber craft about with careless energy, the spray no longer lashed their faces.

The lighthouse crept closer. From the tops of the waves, it was possible to see some of the tiny island, just a sandbar really, held in place by a thatch of scrubby bushes. There was definitely some sort of building, or maybe two, near the tower and Shaun hoped the island was inhabited. He began to imagine the warmth of an open fire, perhaps a steaming mug of soup and a dry bed. There were no lights in the windows, though; it was probably too early for anyone to be up and about.

Rick stirred from his place as they approached the beach. The surf began to boil around them, surging under the Zodiac, and he made his way forward and crouched, ready to leap out. It was unnecessary, though; Steve gunned the outboard to catch a wave and rode it all the way in to the sandy beach, cutting the motor and tilting the propeller out of the water as they slid to a halt. He and Rick slipped over the side and pulled the life raft higher before helping the others out onto the beach.

As Shaun's feet touched the sand, his knees began to shake and the island seemed to heave and sway beneath him. He leaned weakly against Steve and the gentle giant held him up with an arm around his shoulder. 'It's all right, son.' Shaun could feel the deep voice rumbling against him. 'We're here. Just take a minute to catch your breath and then I'll be off.'

'Off? Where to?'

'Can't leave the skipper alone with that maniac, can I?'

Before Shaun could protest, Steve had pushed the Zodiac back into the surf and scrambled over the side. He yanked the starting rope, the engine fired almost immediately, and he swung the craft around deftly just in time to ride up and over the next wave. Shaun glimpsed him twice more, but although the sky was light, the angry sea was dark as slate between the breakers and soon the four children were alone.

13

Stranded on a wisp of sand

SHAUN TRIPPED AND FELL in the sand as they made their way across a wide beach towards wind-wracked scrub that separated them from the buildings. The hand that helped him up was Rick's; leaning on each other for support, they stumbled across piles of seaweed and through the stunted vegetation that covered the sand above the high tide mark. A few metres behind them, Spud and Sam clung together, picking their way around piles of salt-caked driftwood.

Shaun's energy was gone. His clothes were wet, clinging to his thighs and flapping around his ankles, and the wind whipping across the low-lying island cut him to the bone. By the time they reached the first of the houses, he was utterly spent. With an inward slump of disappointment, he realised that the place must be deserted. Although the storm had battered the structures severely, he judged that most of the damage was old; there were gaps in the wooden walls in places and he could see at least one broken window.

The sea had eroded the island right up to the base of the lighthouse and the concrete surrounding the buildings ended in fractured slabs, tilted and undermined by the storm-swells of previous winters. Some distance away, emerging periodically from the surf as it rose and fell with the fading anger of the storm, broken timbers and twisted, rusty metal spoke of other buildings that had already fallen to the advancing sea.

Rick walked up to the door of one house and tried the handle. To Shaun's surprise, it turned and the door swung open. Then, they were inside out of the storm and the relief was almost overwhelming. The wind still rattled windows and banged loose roofing iron, but they were protected from its chilling bite. Shaun could see a vinyl floor, two fridges, a long table.

Making their way from room to room, the four bedraggled friends came to one containing iron beds with lumpy mattresses hanging off rusty springs. Shaun neither knew nor cared what the others were doing; reaching the nearest bed, he collapsed across it and surrendered himself gratefully to unconsciousness. He stirred some time later as somebody gently drew a blanket over him and tucked it in, but he slipped back into a dreamless sleep without knowing who had done it.

Strangely enough, the thing which eventually woke him was the heat. Shaun was feeling uncomfortably warm and tried to push the blanket off himself. He found that he was wrapped so tightly in it that he could barely move his arms. He opened his eyes and saw that the source of the heat was a pile of driftwood blazing in a fireplace on the other side of the room. His parka and a couple of jumpers were draped over chair-backs to dry. There was a grimy window in his field of view and he could see that it was raining heavily. The wind seemed to have died down, but rain thundered on the iron roof of the house and poured from holes in the rusty guttering.

Wriggling free of the blanket, he sat up, feeling slightly dizzy, but otherwise refreshed. The other beds had been used, judging from the jumbled blankets, but they were empty now. The old springs groaned thankfully as he lifted his weight from them and stood up.

A second later, Spud's face appeared around the doorpost. 'Thought I heard something. You slept long enough. Must have been pretty whacked, eh?'

Shaun's eyes were itchy and he rubbed them. 'Mm. Where is everybody?'

'Getting more wood. There's a pile of it in an old shed out the back. Breakfast?'

Shaun suddenly realised he was ravenously hungry. 'Breakfast? What is there?'

Spud grinned. 'Cold baked beans if you're in a hurry. Hot baked beans if you're not. There's some tea bags in there and I'm boiling the kettle right now. No sugar, though. There was half a carton of milk in the fridge, but it's about a million years old and the fridge isn't working anyway. Not a pretty sight. Rick buried it.'

Shaun followed her into the kitchen as she crossed to the old cast-iron stove in the corner. He could see yellow flames flickering behind the grate in the front.

'Hot or cold?' Spud picked up a can from the bench in one hand and an opener with the other.

'Eh?'

'Wake up, Shaun! Baked beans. Hot or cold?'

'Oh, hot.' Shaun shook his head to clear the encroaching fuzziness and sat down. There were no chairs; only two long benches, one on each side of the table. Spud opened the can of beans and dumped them into a saucepan which she placed on the hob. The empty can she added to the three already lined up on the sink. Next to the saucepan, a large aluminium kettle hissed quietly, wisps of steam beginning to curl from the spout. After stirring the beans with a long wooden spoon, and tasting them to see how they were going, Spud came over and sat on the bench next to Shaun. Sliding herself up next to him, she put an arm around his neck and gave it a squeeze.

'Hey, kid,' she said, gently, 'you gave me a fright. We tried to wake you up a while ago and you didn't move. You were so white and cold, and you were breathing so softly, we had to check twice to make sure you were alive.'

Shaun was confused and a bit embarrassed. Not that he minded the arm around his neck, the tousled hair against his forehead, the pressure of her leg against his. Far from it; he had dreamed of something like this more than once. But, he thought, frowning, weren't she and Sam. . . I mean, they were snuggling up together in the chain locker, and in the Zodiac. Well, perhaps she had changed her mind. He took a deep breath and slipped both his arms around her, lowering his mouth towards hers, hoping he would be able to do it right and not make a fool of himself.

'Hey!' Spud stiffened and pulled away from him. 'What was that about?'

'Hey!' Shaun spun around guiltily at the sound of Sam's voice behind him. 'What are you doing?' Sam and Rick had just entered the kitchen, hair dripping wet, with an armload of driftwood each. Sam glared at Shaun, his handsome dark features furrowed with anger. Rick, peering over his shoulder, probably couldn't see what was going on and just looked surprised. Shaun leapt to his feet, his face hot and red.

'I — I'm sorry,' he stammered, facing Spud with pleading eyes. 'I thought — I thought you and me. . . '

'Spud and *you?*' yelped Sam. 'It's Spud and *me*. I'm the one who. . .'

'What?' Spud interrupted. Her eyes, open wide in astonishment, narrowed a second later and pierced the two boys in turn. 'What the hell are you talking about? It's Spud and *nobody!* Did you two think that just because I. . .' She broke off, gasping incredulously. 'Good grief! I'm stranded on an island with a couple of sex maniacs!'

Sam was as puzzled as Shaun. 'You mean. . . are you saying you don't like either of us?' he asked.

'*Like* you?' Spud raised her arms, sighing in exasperation. 'Of course, I *like* you, but I don't *love* you.' She paused, confused. 'Well, really, I suppose I do love you, both of you, but like I love Rick. I'm not *in love* with anyone.'

Rick, who had dumped his load of firewood in the corner of the kitchen, turned around, a strange softness in his eyes. 'You never told me you love me,' he said.

'Course I do, you idiot; you're my brother.' She suddenly stood up and marched purposefully to the stove to rescue the saucepan. 'Men!' she said, shaking her head and pouring the baked beans onto an old, chipped plate. Shaun and Sam looked at each other sheepishly. Rick chuckled to himself and set about stoking the fire in the bottom of the stove.

It stopped raining. One moment the rain was drumming so loudly on the corrugated iron roof that they almost had to shout to make themselves heard across the table, the next they found themselves whispering in the deathly stillness. There was no howling of wind or clattering of loose cladding on the walls. As if from a great distance, they could hear the pounding of surf on the beach and the mewling of seagulls over the house.

They had been discussing their predicament. There was no danger of starving to death; although a diet of baked beans had its drawbacks, there was enough in the cupboards to last several days if they rationed it sensibly. Rainwater from a tank between the two houses was available at a tap over the kitchen sink. It tasted a bit funny and Shaun, familiar with rainwater tanks, wondered privately whether there was a dead bird in it. Rick and Sam had been into the second house on their wood-gathering trip; it was smaller than the one they were in, and in worse condition.

The fact that there were mattresses on the beds and baked beans in the cupboard convinced them that the island was visited fairly regularly (though not frequently, they had to admit, remembering the age of the milk). While it had been raining, the only thing to do was to make themselves as comfortable as possible and wait. Once the rain stopped, however, it took them about five seconds to decide it was time to explore their island.

There was a bit of wind — nothing like the gale they had endured for the last twelve hours, but strong enough to ruffle their hair and cold enough to send them back inside for their coats. The sea, though, seemed to be moved by forces from below; it still heaved and roiled like liquid lead, dumping short, heavy breakers onto the beach. It seemed to give off a kind of haze that all but obscured the mainland a few kilometres away. Together, the four stepped off the ramshackle wooden verandah and began their examination of the island.

Immediately before them was the lighthouse. It was shorter than Shaun had remembered from his first sight of it. It was painted in horizontal red and white bands and seemed to be made of metal, not stone as he had imagined. They climbed onto the concrete foundation and felt the sides, marred and bubbled in places by rust. A door in the side was securely padlocked. There was a pipe leading from the ground to the railing high above, where the light was.

Sam had an idea he could climb it and somehow tamper with the light, thus attracting attention from the mainland, but Rick quickly vetoed this. They were safe where they were, he said, and if another storm blew up, ships would be in danger if the light was not working properly. Besides, he added with a mischievous grin, if Sam fell and broke his neck, Spud would never forgive him. Rick got a punch on the arm from his sister for that.

They picked their way through the tumbled remains of old concrete foundations and out along the beach. Occasionally, they came across pieces of dis-carded household items and speculated on who had lived here and where they were now.

'You can see why they left,' observed Spud. 'I reckon the island used to be a lot bigger. Look over there, where those posts stick up out of the water. I bet there was some kind of building there.'

The centre of the island, behind the houses, was thickly covered with tangled, woody scrub, most of it too prickly to penetrate. There were sea birds of various kinds huddled in sandy burrows and stony nests amongst the bushes, and Shaun even thought he saw a penguin wriggle out of sight into a thicket. The birds must have agreed with the children that the storm had blown itself out. By the time the four had made a circuit of the island, an exercise that took all of ten minutes, the indetermi-nate backdrop of grey sea and grey sky was dotted by white and black as the birds wheeled and cried above them.

Following the flight of one particularly large gull above the house, Shaun's eyes were suddenly ar-rested by a familiar shape.

'Look!' he shouted. The others all looked, in vari-ous directions, with uncomprehending expressions. 'No, over there. That antenna.'

'The TV antenna?' asked Rick. 'I don't think it's connected. At least, I didn't see a TV anywhere.'

'It's not TV,' announced Shaun in triumph. 'We've got one at home on Turtleshell. It's the telephone.'

'You sure?' queried Spud. 'Telephones don't have antennas.'

'Some places they do,' agreed Sam. 'Where it's too far or too hard to run a cable.'

'Well, what are we waiting for?' Rick started running towards the tower. 'Let's see where it goes.'

They began at the foot of the antenna tower, any doubt dispelled by the sight of the orange Telecom logo, and followed an overhead cable to the back of the second house. Peering through the window nearest where the cable was attached, they saw that it was an office of sorts, with a map on the wall and, yes, a telephone in the middle of the dusty desk. Entering the house, they found that the door of the office was locked, and debated whether to break it open.

'I'm sure the owners wouldn't mind,' stated Rick. 'My dad would probably dock me a month's pocket money to pay for the damage, but I reckon it's worth it.'

'Don't have to break it open,' offered Sam. He turned to Shaun. 'Remember what I told you about the credit card trick?'

Shaun knit his brow, thinking, then remembered. 'Yes, well, I reckon I left home without my American Express. What about the rest of you?'

Sam ignored him. Stooping, he hooked his fingers under a broken piece of the old vinyl floor covering and ripped off a piece about as big as his hand. Inserting it between the door and the jamb at the same height as the lock, he wiggled it up and down, slowly sliding it forward.

'There!' he crowed, as the catch gave with a click and the door swung open.

Rick slapped him on the back. 'Nice one, mate!'

Eagerly, the four friends crowded around the desk and they could all hear the dial tone as Spud picked up the phone. 'Who should I call?' she asked.

Rick looked at Sam. 'What say we start with the police?' he said.

Sam shrugged. 'Worth a try, I guess.'

14

Somehow things are different

THE LAST TIME SHAUN HAD SLEPT, he had been stranded on a wisp of sand in the middle of St Vincent's Gulf; now the warmth of the radiator in his bedroom was making him very drowsy. Dinner was over and Sam's mother was expected to arrive at any moment. The boys were passing the time switching channels on the TV, trying to catch any news coverage of their rescue. Both of them were having trouble keeping their eyes open.

They had already seen it on three different stations and Shaun knew it by heart. One news team had been quick off the mark, arriving over the island in their helicopter not long after the Edithburgh police had reached them by boat. The story usually began with a brief introduction by the newsreader: 'A successful conclusion, today, to the abduction of four

Adelaide teenagers when they dragged themselves ashore on a tiny island after being shipwrecked during last night's violent storm.'

Aerial footage of Troubridge Island was followed by pictures, taken after the chopper had landed, of the young people being carried to the rescue boat, wrapped in blankets. They had raised tired smiles for the camera, but looked much more exhausted than Shaun remembered feeling at the time.

The helicopter ride back across the Gulf had been fun. The reception at the other end had been emotional. Watching the news reports, Shaun had squirmed a bit when the camera zoomed in on his tear-stained face, just visible over his mother's shoulder. Rick and Spud's father had been there, too, embracing his children, and there hadn't been a dry eye in that little group, either.

Finding his children gone when he arrived home from work in the early hours of the morning, Rick's dad had begun phoning all their friends. Shaun and Sam were found to be missing, too, and the police had been called. Shaun's parents had driven down from Turtleshell, being greeted on arrival with the news that the children had made contact from Troubridge Island, although the rest of the story was still unknown at that stage. They had made it to the airport just in time to meet the incoming helicopter.

Sam's mother, Mrs Dobson, had to come from Leigh Creek by bus, a ten-hour trip, and had not yet arrived. Sam had pretended not to mind, but Shaun could see from the way he looked at the other families that he really did. Mrs Walker put her arm around Sam's shoulder and Shaun was pleased to see his friend accept the comforting squeeze as they ran the gauntlet of cameras and microphones on their way to the cars.

Safe and warm now, Sam was slumped in an armchair with his eyes closed and Shaun was lying on his bed, lulled nearly to sleep by the murmur of the television. They were roused by a high-pitched 'beep' from the intercom. Sam stirred, rubbing his eyes tiredly as Shaun crossed the room to answer it.

'Sorry to disturb you, Shaun,' said Mrs Walker's voice, 'but Sam's mother has just arrived.'

'Okay. We'll be up in a minute.'

Sam reached the house first and, by the time Shaun entered the living room, Mrs Dobson had her arms wrapped firmly around her son. She rocked back and forth, alternately scolding and then comforting him.

'You little rascal! You get yourself in more strife than Ned Kelly, you do! I dunno, God must have a mob of angels full time just watching out for you. I reckon he's sick of hearing from me about it; I been at him non-stop since you shot through. Ah, you little ratbag, do you know what you put me through? I been worried sick. Your father, too. Spite of everything, he loves you, you know. Kept telling me he was sorry you ran off because of him. He wanted to take time off and come down with me to pick you up, but he's just started that job and I told him he better not. Oh, but I'm glad you're okay, you rotten little beggar.'

Eventually, she let him go in order to mop her eyes with a handkerchief and he escaped to the safety of the couch, punching the 'on' button of the TV controller as he went. Shaun's parents were staying overnight in the Walkers' spare room, and there was something of a reunion between them and Emma Dobson. Mrs Walker brought coffee for the adults and hot milk and honey for the boys, then Sam called for silence as he found a channel just starting a mid-evening news update.

'In a dramatic sequel to the rescue of four school children from Troubridge Island earlier today, Customs officers boarded a Taiwanese vessel near Port Lincoln, seizing a number of wooden crates and taking three Adelaide men into custody. One of the men is believed to be the owner of a prawn trawler found drifting in St Vincent's Gulf this afternoon.'

It was oddly thrilling to see the *Ginny Ann* again. She appeared on the television screen, wallowing in the ocean swell, viewed from different angles as the news helicopter circled her. Her stern was under water and she was listing heavily, but she was still afloat and Shaun felt a kind of pride, like he did when his father came second in the wood chopping at the Show.

'I wonder what will happen to the skipper and Steve?' he said.

'Be pretty tough for them, I'd think,' replied Mr Walker. 'Bird smuggling's bad enough, but once it turned into kidnapping, well, I'd say they're in hot water. And rightly so, too.'

'Well, they didn't really have much choice,' protested Shaun. 'Jacobson had a gun. He made them do it. And anyway, they didn't really kidnap us: we stowed away and they just locked us up to protect us from Jacobson.'

'Yeah,' put in Sam. 'We told the cops Jacobson was the bad guy. We told them Steve and the skipper were kind to us. I reckon the cops believed us. I hope they let them go.'

'Me, too,' said Shaun. 'I feel sorry for them. The skipper's a nice bloke. He's got a wife and daughter, I think. Just lives up the road from here. I don't know how he got mixed up with all that stuff. Jacobson must have had some kind of hold over him.'

'Needed the money, I suppose,' agreed Shaun's dad. 'Thought he could get away with it. Probably would have if it wasn't for you nosey kids! Strike a light! What the hell did you think you were doing, getting involved like that? You could have been killed!'

Shaun's mother put a hand on her husband's arm. 'They weren't, though, were they? They were in good hands and they learned a lesson or two.' She smiled. 'Besides, they're not the only teenagers ever to try upholding the law by themselves. Was it you or your brother that threatened the new vet with a shotgun when you thought he was stealing one of the horses?'

Shaun's father grinned sheepishly. 'It was my brother. All right,' he conceded, reluctantly, 'I got the gun from the house, but he pointed it. That was different, though. It was on our own property. Dad should have warned us someone was coming to collect her.'

Mrs Dobson had arranged to stay with an old friend in Birkenhead, so Shaun helped Sam collect his few belongings and take them out to Mr Walker's car. Then Shaun's parents went with him down to the granny flat where he discovered that he was not too old to enjoy being hugged and tucked into bed.

'Night,' he murmured as they turned off the light and quietly shut the door, but he was asleep before they reached the house.

Shaun was up and dressed early, and they all drove down to the bus station before school to see Sam off. Rick and Spud were there, and Sam seemed surprised that they had all made the effort to come.

'Course we came, you duffer,' laughed Spud, giving him a hug. 'Couldn't let you get away without saying goodbye.'

Shaun wanted to hug his friend, too, but there were too many people around. He stuck out his hand and Sam shook it vigorously. 'Told you we might have some fun together,' said Shaun.

Sam grinned. 'Yeah. We had fun, didn't we? Come

and visit me. See what we can get up to next time!'

Rick stepped forward and offered his hand. 'Glad I met you,' he said as Sam returned his grip. 'I. . . look, I'm sorry I. . .'

'It's all right. I know,' said Sam. He suddenly became embarrassed and turned towards the bus, brushing something from his eye. Pausing on the bottom step, he turned around again. 'Be good!' he called. 'Don't do anything I wouldn't do!'

'Don't do half of what he *would* do, either!' warned Emma Dobson as she hustled her son up the steps and down the aisle to his seat.

They were greeted at the school gate like heroes.

'Saw you on telly!' shouted Dave, above the clamour. 'Talk about wall-to-wall cops! Hey, what'd they book you for?'

'Nothing,' replied Rick, leading the crowd into the corridor and throwing his bag into his locker. 'They just made us sit down in a room at the airport and tell them what had happened. Then, we went home.'

'Bet they book you for something,' insisted Jason. 'You were right: Shaun's Abo mate was trouble after all.'

Rick turned slowly and his dark eyes bored into Jason's before shifting to skewer Dave. Then, he sighed and made his way back through the press of curious onlookers. 'Come on, Shaun,' he said on his way out into the yard. 'Let's get some fresh air. It smells bad in there.'

As they crossed the asphalt, heading for the oval, Spud caught up with them and slipped between them, hooking an arm through each of theirs. Shaun looked at her in surprise. 'Hey, Shaun,' she said, 'I *am* fond of you, you know. Honest.'

They walked like that for a while, the three of them, until the bell rang and they turned back towards the buildings.

There was something Shaun had been wanting to ask for months. Maybe now was the time. 'Spud,' he began, as they reached the edge of the grass, 'what's your real name?'

'Come on,' she replied, giving him a stern look that really didn't work very well. 'I'm not *that* fond of you! Yet.'